MW00991380

STEADFAST
AND
IMMOVABLE

STRIVING FOR SPIRITUAL MATURITY

ROBERT L. MILLET

Deseret Book Company
Salt Lake City, Utah

Library of Congress Cataloging-in-Publication Data

Millet, Robert L.
   Steadfast and immovable : striving for spiritual maturity / Robert L. Millet.
      p.   cm.
   Includes bibliographical references and index.
   ISBN 0-87579-635-4
   1. Christian life—Mormon authors.   2. Church of Jesus Christ of Latter-day Saints—Doctrines.   3. Mormon Church—Doctrines.
I. Title.
BX8656.M545   1992
248.4'89332—dc20   92-18727
                                                                CIP

Printed in the United States of America

10   9   8   7   6   5   4   3   2   1

Therefore, I would that ye should be steadfast and immovable, always abounding in good works, that Christ, the Lord God Omnipotent, may seal you his, that you may be brought to heaven, that ye may have everlasting salvation and eternal life.

—Mosiah 5:15

Contents

Preface

The prophet-editor Mormon writes that Helaman had two sons. "He gave unto the eldest the name of Nephi, and unto the youngest, the name of Lehi. And they began to grow up unto the Lord." (Helaman 3:21.) What interesting words: "They began to grow up unto the Lord." One can only wonder what Mormon intended by that remark. Is he implying that the two sons began to sense, at an early age, what matters most in life? Did he mean that they were eager to please their parents and even more anxious to please the Lord in all they said and did? Could it be that from their youth they sought for and enjoyed the gifts of the Spirit, walked in the light of that Spirit, and centered their minds and hearts on things of righteousness?

The fact is, the Lord calls us to do the same, to grow up in him, to mature spiritually to the point where we see things from an elevated perspective, things as they really are. The Prophet Joseph Smith prayed at the time of the dedication of the Kirtland Temple: "And do thou grant, Holy Father, that all those who shall worship in this house may be taught words of wisdom out of the best books, and that they may seek learning even by study, and also by faith, as thou hast said; and *that they may grow up in thee, and receive a fulness of the Holy Ghost,* and be organized according to thy laws, and be prepared to obtain every needful thing." (D&C 109:14–15; italics added.) We are sent to earth to mature, to grow up and to be added upon. The gospel of Jesus Christ is the power of God unto life and salvation, the power by which we grow up in the Lord, the means whereby we become in time steadfast and immovable.

One of the ironies associated with spiritual maturity is that we must start over, start from the beginning, become as little children, before we can grow up and proceed along the gospel path. The angel explained to King Benjamin that every person must put off the natural man and become a saint through the atonement of Christ the Lord, become "as a child, submissive, meek, humble, patient, full of love, willing to submit to all things which the Lord seeth fit to inflict upon him, even as a child doth submit to his father." (Mosiah 3:19.) In contrast to the world's ways, gospel maturity is accomplished through submission, through surrender. It is evident in the lives of those who have overcome self, who have postponed the gratification of present pleasures and chosen instead to seek for peace in this life and eternal life in the world to come. Those who have "chosen that good part" (Luke 10:42) know, like Paul, that "eye hath not seen, nor ear heard, neither have entered into the heart of man, the things which God hath prepared for them that love him" (1 Corinthians 2:9).

Those who are steadfast and immovable have received the Holy Ghost and taken the Spirit as their guide: they have committed themselves to a course of loyalty to the true Church and devotion to the faith of their fathers. Like Nephi of old, they give no heed to the tauntings and ridicule of persons who whelp and sneer from the large and spacious building. (1 Nephi 8:33.) The mature stand in holy places and remain unmoved (D&C 87:8); theirs is a steady, consistent effort in a world of constantly shifting views and values.

This book deals with spiritual maturity, with growing up in the Lord, with acquiring those attributes and that strength which allow us, in a world without absolutes, to be steadfast and immovable. In its preparation I am indebted to many people — students, friends, faculty colleagues, and teachers — many of whom have exemplified the principles discussed herein. I express special thanks to Lori Soza, a capable and conscientious secretary and assistant, who has read each chapter, made helpful suggestions, and in general prepared the manuscript for publication. I alone am responsible, however, for the conclusions drawn from the evidence cited. This book is a private endeavor and not an official publication of The Church of Jesus Christ of Latter-day Saints or of Brigham Young University. I write of these things not from a position of personal spiritual maturity but rather as one who has sought understanding on the matter and, more important, one who longs with all his heart to so arrive one day. For me, as with most of mankind, the ideal is yet to become an unblemished reality. But I believe in the ideal and hope that this work will motivate others, with me, to strive toward its realization.

Chapter One

Dealing with Difficult Questions

Ponder for a moment upon what God has revealed in these last days. Through Joseph Smith and his successors, the Lord Almighty has seen fit to make known the answers to some of life's most perplexing questions: Where did I come from? Why am I here? Where am I going when I leave here? As Latter-day Saints we are able to talk intelligently about doctrinal matters that are completely mysterious to those outside the faith, some matters which must sound like the gibberish of alien tongues to those who have not received the gift of the Holy Ghost. The nature of God, life in a premortal and a postmortal existence, the continuation of the family unit into eternity—these and a myriad of other topics are but illustrative of the unutterable knowledge and intelligence that have been poured out upon the heads of the Lord's people in this final gospel dispensation. These great truths are uniquely Latter-day Saint; they are a part of our heritage and constitute the doctrinal reservoir that helps to make of the Latter-day Saints "a peculiar people." (1 Peter 2:9.) We have so much.

In fact, we're spoiled! We have the answers to so many questions, the solutions to so many of the world's vexing issues, the only meaningful suggestion for peace in a troubled world—peace here and peace hereafter. In fact, we have so many answers to so many religious questions that some of us expect to have them all. And it's downright unsettling when we happen upon some dilemma for which no answer is forthcoming, something which is at best unclear or at worst unrevealed. It is the nature of mankind to seek for closure, to strive to fill in the blanks. That is as it should be. Our souls reach out for answers. We are eternal creatures living in a mortal world, spiritual beings undergoing a temporal experience. The veil of forgetfulness purposely and purposefully denies us access to many things we once knew, many parts of a rather intricate and complex puzzle. Even with all that has been delivered by prophets and apostles, by wise men and women, and by the spirit of inspiration, there are and will be questions. Difficult questions, nagging questions, questions that are troublesome and at times seemingly unanswerable.

It is important to note that there is no evil in having questions, no harm in wondering and asking and inquiring. No person, Latter-day Saint or otherwise, ought to feel guilty because he or she has questions. Such is perfectly normal, a part of the plan. If we already possessed the solutions to all the traumas and the formulae for all the paradoxes, there would be little purpose and certainly little fulfillment to be had in this second estate. Success in life and spiritual maturity, depend not upon whether we have questions but rather with how we deal with them. Whatever the nature of our queries, there are both counterproductive and productive, both fruitful and unfruitful means of engaging them. We shall in this chapter consider some examples of each.

Some Counterproductive Approaches

There are several approaches to solving our doctrinal or historical problems that do not prove to be extremely helpful. Indeed, they are and will always be hazardous to our spiritual health. Some years ago my family and I moved from a part of the country we had come to love dearly. I was asked to assume a new assignment in the Church Educational System, which required a relocation. We had been in our new home for only a few weeks when I received a telephone call late one Sunday evening. The woman on the other end of the line was deeply distraught. "Brother Millet," she said, "this is Sister Johnson."

"Yes, Sister Johnson," I responded. I had known the Johnson family quite well. Brother Johnson had been a member of the bishopric in their ward and Sister Johnson had served in the presidencies of both the Primary and Relief Society, while I had served as a member of the stake presidency in that area. I had been in their home several times, had enjoyed dinners and social gatherings with them, had known of their dedicated Church service, and believed them to be one of the most settled and secure Latter-day Saint families anywhere. They had joined the Church after having been found and taught by the missionaries some ten years earlier. They were themselves extremely missionary-minded and had been instrumental in leading several families to baptism. But there was obvious pain in Sister Johnson's voice. I tried to be positive and asked, "What can I do for you?"

"I desperately need your help," she said. "My husband is about to leave the Church."

Her statement nearly took my breath away. "Leave the Church?" I asked. "What do you mean?"

She explained that her husband's brother, a nonmember

who had opposed their baptism, had for several months been sending bitter anti-Mormon propaganda through the mail. She said that at first her husband had ignored it but after a few weeks he began perusing it out of sheer curiosity. "I began to notice a gradual change in Bill," she stated. She pointed out that he had become argumentative and uncooperative at Church, touchy and ill at ease at home, and just plain unsettled in his demeanor. "He has a lot of questions, Brother Millet," she added, "and I'm afraid that if he doesn't get them answered pretty soon, we'll lose him."

"How can I help?" I inquired.

"He wants to talk with you," Sister Johnson came back.

"Good," I said, "put him on the line."

"Oh no," she said, "he wants to meet with you in person."

I replied that such a meeting would be perfectly fine with me but that we were now some ten or twelve hours driving distance from each other. I suggested that if this was the only way to deal with his questions, if his concerns could not be addressed by someone in their area, then we should set a time when we might get together.

"He's already on his way," she then observed. "He left a couple of hours ago. Would you please meet with him? He'll be at the institute by 9:00 a.m."

I was a bit startled, but I quickly assured Sister Johnson that I would be more than happy to meet with him and do what I could.

Brother Johnson wasn't the only one who didn't sleep that night. I tossed and turned through the night, arose several times, and retired to the living room to pray for guidance. The morning came faster than I had wished, and my stomach churned as I contemplated what the meeting might entail. Sister Johnson was quite accurate in her prediction: her husband arrived a little after nine o'clock. She was also quite accurate in her description of her husband's condition. He had a fallen countenance, a dark look in his eyes, and in general a rather gloomy appearance; this simply was not the man I had known before. He had lost the Spirit and was like a broken man, a person who had lost his innocence, who had lost his way. We knelt and prayed together, and I pleaded with the Lord to dispel the spirit of gloom and doubt and endow us with the spirit of light and understanding. The answer to that prayer came eventually but only after a long and difficult struggle. As is so often the case, Brother Johnson had been confronted with scores of questions on authority, on the Church's claim to being Christian, on temple rites, on doctrinal teachings of specific Church leaders, on changes in scripture or Church practice, etc., etc. An endless list. I responded to every issue, suggesting an answer if such was possible. In some cases, the answer was simply a call for faith, an invitation to pray or pray again about whether Joseph Smith was a prophet of God, whether his successors have worn the same mantle of authority, and whether the Church is divinely led today. I sensed, however, that there was something deeper, something beneath the surface issues that he was raising, something that was festering and eating away at his soul like a cancer. It took me almost eight hours to discover what that something was.

When Brother and Sister Johnson were first taught the gospel and introduced to the Book of Mormon, one of the missionaries — no doubt well-meaning but short-sighted — had said something like, "Now, Brother and Sister Johnson, the Book of Mormon is true. It came from God to Joseph Smith. And you can know for yourselves that it is true by praying about it. But, the fact is, there are so many archaeological

evidences of its truthfulness these days, it almost isn't necessary to pray about it!" The statement sounded convincing
enough. Brother Johnson bought into that line of reasoning
and—short-sighted on his part—never took occasion to pray
with real intent about the Book of Mormon. When anti-
Mormon materials suggested that there were not as many
external evidences of the Nephite or Jaredite civilizations as
he had been told previously, his whole world collapsed. If
the Book of Mormon wasn't true, he reasoned, then Joseph
Smith was not a prophet. If Joseph Smith was not a
prophet. . . . And so on. One fateful step led to another. And
now he was ready to throw it all away, unfortunately because
his testimony was not substantive, his doctrinal foundation
was weak and shifting. And he had been unwilling to exercise
sufficient faith and patience to refocus upon the things that
really count—in this case the message or content of the Book
of Mormon.

It was a relief to finally get down to the core issue. I
explained to him that we were now up against the wall of
faith and that the only issue to be decided was whether or
not he was willing to pay the price to know the truth. I asked
some hard questions: Did you ever know that this work is
true? What was your witness based on? What has this doubt-
ing and this vexation of the soul done to your wife and children? Does the bitter spirit you have felt during the last few
months come from God? And then I asked: Are you willing
to throw it all away, to jettison all that is good and ennobling
because your foundation was deficient? He paused, reflected
again on the painful and poignant strugglings he had under-
gone, but then added that he wanted more than anything to
feel once more what he had felt ten years earlier. I stressed
to him the need for staying with simple and solid doctrinal

matters, particularly in regard to the Book of Mormon and the Restoration, for focusing upon the things of greatest worth, for following the same course of study and pondering and prayer that he had followed during his initial investigation of the Church. I challenged him never to yield to the temptation to "jump ship" when he encountered things he didn't understand, especially when there were so many things he did understand. It was a sweet experience to watch the light of faith and trust come back into his countenance and into his life.

I have detailed this experience because it highlights the tragic reality that too often people are prone to "jump ship," to forsake family and friends and faith—to give it all up—because there is an unanswered question or an unresolved dilemma. It also points up graphically that our spiritual lives must be built upon the proper foundations if we are to be steady in our discipleship and mature in our faith. (We will discuss this point later.)

Let me briefly refer to another experience. Several years ago I became acquainted with a lovely young family who joined the Church—a mother, a father, and two children. They seemed a perfect conversion, people who loved the Church, were eager to jump in with both feet, and anxious to share their newfound way of life with others. Sister Brown was quickly absorbed into the Primary, while Brother Brown became fast friends with members of the elders quorum. It was after they had been in the Church for well over a year that Brother Brown came to see me at my office one day. He expressed his love for the Church as well as the thrill he felt at seeing his family deeply rooted in Mormonism. Then he shared with me something that I never would have supposed—that he did not really have a witness of Joseph Smith's prophetic calling. He said, in essence: "Bob, I love the gospel with all my heart. I know that this is the true Church. There's no question in my mind about it. This is what I want for my family, now and always. But I have a problem, one that won't go away: I just don't know that Joseph Smith was a prophet."

He then commented on how silly such a thing must sound to me, that is, to accept and embrace the revelation and at the same time be unable to accept and acknowledge the revelator. He said, "I've prayed and prayed and prayed for a testimony of Joseph Smith, but I still can't say that I know he was called of God. I sincerely believe that he was a great and good man and that in the purest sense he was inspired of God. But I just don't know for sure that he was a prophet. What do I do?" This was a bit unusual to me. From all I could discern, there was no duplicity, no cynicism, no skepticism, only simple and pure uncertainty; he wanted so badly to know, but he didn't know. We worked together on this problem for years. We read books on Joseph Smith; we fasted together; we prayed together. In all that time, Brother Brown remained true and faithful. He labored in the auxiliaries of the Church and for a time served as an elders quorum president. He and his family were active and involved in every way that could be expected of them. Our families grew quite close, and we often spent time talking about life and its challenges, about the central place of the gospel in our lives, and about where we would be if we were not members of the Church.

In time we moved from the area. Several years later I received a telephone call from Brother Brown. "Bob," he said excitedly, "I have something to tell you. I have a testimony of Joseph Smith. These feelings have been growing within me for several months now, but I can finally stand and say that I know. I *know!*" I wept with him as we talked about the peace of mind he had gained, as we discussed this most recent phase of his lengthy but steady conversion. It had taken almost eight years for him to come to know, but in the interim he had done all that was expected of him. I have a witness as to how much the Lord loves Brother Brown and all the other Brother and Sister Browns who have the spiritual stamina and moral courage to hang on, to hold to the rod, even when they are not absolutely certain about the destination of the path they traverse. Surely that is what the Savior meant when he counseled us: "Search diligently, pray always, and be believing, and all things shall work together for your good, if ye walk uprightly and remember the covenant wherewith ye have covenanted one with another." (D&C 90:24.)

Another example of a counterproductive approach to obtaining answers is going to the wrong people for help. A man and his wife whom I knew quite well joined the Church in the southern part of the United States. After a year's involvement with the Church, they traveled to Washington, D. C., to receive the blessings of the temple. On returning home, the man had several unanswered questions about the temple, and so he contacted his former Protestant minister and arranged a meeting. The minister was of course more than willing to oblige him and especially eager to give answers to his queries regarding Mormon temples. As one might suppose, the family left the LDS Church within a matter of weeks and returned to their former church. Simply stated, one does not go to Caiaphas or Pilate to learn about Jesus. One goes to Peter, James, or John, those who knew the Master intimately. One does not go to the enemies of Joseph Smith or the critics of the Church if one sincerely wants to gain understanding concerning the faith. Wisdom suggests that one does not take one's doubts to a known doubter and expect to receive peace of mind.

Each of us is under obligation to search and ponder upon the issues ourselves, to do our best to learn by study and by faith the answers to our concerns. (See D&C 9:7–9.) Every member of this church has a direct channel to our Heavenly Father; there is no one between us and God. Every person who has been baptized and confirmed has a right to the companionship and guidance of the Holy Ghost, the Comforter, even that Spirit of Truth, which knows all things. (See D&C 42:17; Moses 6:61.) In addition, members of a ward or branch can readily take their concerns to their priesthood leaders—their bishop or branch president. If he does not know the answer to the question, he can inquire of the stake president. If the stake president is unable to address the concern and feels it advisable to do so, he may inquire of the general authorities of the Church.

People ought to feel free to ask their questions. If an answer is to be had, it can be obtained through proper channels. There is a temptation, when we are troubled by a particular matter, to spend inordinate amounts of time researching it. Some things have just not been revealed, and thus to devote ourselves endlessly to the discovery of what in essence is the undiscoverable (at least for now) is counterproductive. It's almost a waste of time, especially when our efforts could be so much more profitably expended in studying upon and reinforcing the things that *have* been given of God. There is a remarkable phenomenon to which we ought to pay particular attention, one to which I can bear especial witness: Constant review of basic principles constantly brings increased spiritual insight. "Those who preach by the power of the Holy Ghost," Elder Bruce R. McConkie explained, "use the scriptures as their basic source of knowledge and doctrine. They begin with what the Lord has before revealed to other inspired men. But it is the practice of the Lord *to give added knowledge to those upon whose hearts the true meaning and intents of the scriptures have been impressed.* Many great doctrinal revelations come to those who preach from the scriptures. When they are in tune with the Infinite, *the Lord lets them know, first, the full and complete meaning of the scriptures they are expounding, and then he ofttimes expands their views so that new truths flood in upon them, and they learn added things* that those who do not follow such a course can never know." (*Promised Messiah,* pp. 515–16; italics added.)

Stated differently, we reduce the realm of the unknown not by wandering in it but rather by delighting in and expanding our knowledge of what God has already revealed. It is a soul-satisfying experience to be reading Topic A and then to have our minds caught away to consider Topic B. Indeed, serious, consistent, prayerful consideration and reflection upon the *institutional* revelations (the standard works and the words of the living prophets) result in *individual* revelations, including—should the Lord determine that it is appropriate and we are ready to receive the same—the answers to our more difficult questions. Those answers may come as a specific response to a specific concern, or they may come in the form of a comforting and peaceful assurance that all is well, that God is in his heaven, that the work in which we are engaged is true, that specifics will be made known in the Lord's due time. Either way, answers do come. They really do, but only when we go to the right source.

Some people trip over a false assumption whenever they encounter hard doctrine or tough issues or uncover something they consider to be a painful discovery. After they have

searched and looked and sifted and sorted through all they
can find, after they have made what they believe to be their
best effort to solve the problem, they conclude that because
they do not understand, then no one else does either. That's
quite a presumptuous conclusion, but it is, nevertheless, a
surprisingly common one. Humility demands a different
stance. Meekness forces us to acknowledge that there just
might be someone brighter or more experienced than we are,
or maybe even someone who has struggled with this issue
before. Common sense suggests that the odds are against
absolute originality in regard to our specific concern. And
even if it is possible that we have indeed unearthed something
that no other mortal has ever encountered, still, there are
good and wise people in our midst who have been blessed
with the gifts of the Spirit — with discernment, with revelation,
with wisdom and judgment — to assist us in putting all things
in proper perspective.

Unfortunately, some members of the Church do not learn
this lesson and thus wander in the morass of a sort of
dwindling belief. Having yielded themselves to the spirit of
skepticism, having become thereby an easy prey to those who
proselyte others to share their doubts, some members of the
Church begin to read, as President Joseph F. Smith warned,
by the lamp of their own conceit, to interpret what they know
and experience by rules of their own contriving. (*Gospel Doctrine,* p. 373.) If not checked by repentance and sincere submission, such persons can lose their faith and thus their vision.
When a person refuses to exercise faith — to have a hope in
that which is unseen but true (Alma 32:21), he thereby denies
himself access to the spiritual world, another realm of reality
entirely. His vision of things is at best deficient and at worst
perverse; he does not see things "as they really are." (Jacob

4:13; compare D&C 93:24.) Such a view of reality precludes one's apprehension of the unseen and one's desire to grasp the unknown. In time there will be no place in such persons' tightly enclosed epistemological system for such matters as spirit and revelation and prophecy. The doubter—the one whose faith centers in what may be seen and heard and felt through natural means only—errs grossly through generalizing beyond his own experiences. What he has not experienced, he assumes no one else can. Because he does not know, no one knows (see Alma 30:48); because he is past feeling, surely no one else has felt; because he lacks internal evidence concerning the things of God, unquestionably the evidence amassed by every believing soul is either insufficient or naively misinterpreted. Those who dare not believe dare not allow others to believe.

A related tendency by some is to parade their doubts, to suppose by "coming out of the closet" with an announcement of all things that trouble them that they shall somehow either feel better about their difficulties or identify and join hands with others who similarly struggle. One need not suffer alone. Help is available, within fairly easy reach. To be quite direct, however, precious little good comes from "hanging out our dirty laundry," from making public proclamations about one's inner anxieties—little good to the individual, and little good to groups of people. Such things merely feed doubt and perpetuate it. "Why are a few members," asked Elder Neal A. Maxwell, "who somewhat resemble the ancient Athenians, so eager to hear some new doubt or criticism? (see Acts 17:21). Just as some weak members slip across a state line to gamble, a few go out of their way to have their doubts titillated. Instead of nourishing their faith, they are gambling 'offshore' with their fragile faith. To the question 'Will ye also go away?' these few would reply, 'Oh, no, we merely want a weekend pass in order to go to a casino for critics or a clubhouse for cloakholders.' Such easily diverted members are not disciples but fair-weather followers. Instead," Elder Maxwell concluded, "true disciples are rightly described as steadfast and immovable, pressing forward with 'a perfect brightness of hope' (2 Nephi 31:20; see also D&C 49:23)." (In Conference Report, Oct. 1988, p. 40.)

Again, one of the signs of our spiritual maturity is how we handle difficult issues or controversial matters. A Latter-day Saint may have a genuine difference of opinion from one or more leaders of the Church or may not agree with a particular doctrine or practice of the Church. Those may be matters with which he or she labors for many years before a resolution is forthcoming. But for the loyal and devoted Saint they are private struggles of the soul, never intended to become public crusades. To proceed otherwise — to promote differing views, to publish differences with the Church, to sensationalize what we feel to be error or misdeed in the Church — is to border on personal apostasy. "We could conceive of a man," President George Q. Cannon observed, "honestly differing in opinion from the Authorities of the Church and yet not be an apostate; but we could not conceive of a man publishing these differences of opinion and seeking by arguments, sophistry and special pleading to enforce them upon the people to produce division and strife and to place the acts and counsels of the Authorities of the Church, if possible, in a wrong light, and not be an apostate, for such conduct was apostasy as we understood the term.

"We further said that while a man might honestly differ in opinion from the Authorities through a want of understanding, he had to be exceedingly careful how he acted in relation to such differences, or the adversary would take advantage of him, and he would soon become imbued with the spirit of apostasy and be found fighting against God and the authority which He had placed here to govern His Church." (*Gospel Truth,* p. 493.)

Some Productive Approaches

Questions will arise in each of our individual spheres, at least as long as we are learning and growing and seeking to understand what life is about. With some questions we may simply be able to ask ourselves: "Does this really matter? Is this issue important enough to worry myself about? Is it worth the effort?" We have only so much time and energy in this life; we would do well to ignore, where possible, the unimportant, to avoid getting caught up, as someone has suggested, in the thick of thin things. As a professor of religion at Brigham Young University, it has been fascinating to me (and sometimes a bit discouraging) to find what some students grapple with. This one just has to know the exact size of Kolob. That one won't rest until he has calculated the precise dimensions of the celestial city seen by John the Revelator. Others wrestle with the present resting place of the ark of the covenant or Joseph Smith's seerstone. "There is so much to learn," Elder Bruce R. McConkie has written in an open letter to honest truth seekers, "about the great eternal verities which shape our destiny that it seems a shame to turn our attention everlastingly to the minutiae and insignificant things. So often questions like this are asked: 'I know it is not essential to my salvation, but I would really like to know how many angels can dance on the head of a pin and if it makes any difference whether the pin is made of brass or bronze?' There is such a thing as getting so tied up with little fly specks on the great canvas which depicts the whole plan of salvation that we lose sight of what the life and the light and the glory of eternal reward are all about. (See, e.g., Matt. 23:23–25.) There is such a thing as virtually useless knowledge, the acquisition of which won't make one iota of difference to the destiny of the kingdom or the salvation of its subjects." (*Doctrines of the Restoration,* p. 232.)

In teaching some of my religion classes, I have occasionally said that it is as important to know what we do not know as it is to know what we know. Further, to quarrel and dispute over the unknown and the unrevealed is fruitless and absolutely unnecessary. In that spirit, it is fundamentally necessary for us occasionally to say, "I don't know." Part of our spiritual maturity is reflected in our ability to deal with ambiguity, to handle uncertainty. President Joseph F. Smith wisely pointed out that "the religion of the heart, the unaffected and simple communion which we should hold with God, is the highest safeguard of the Latter-day Saints. It is no discredit to our intelligence or to our integrity to say frankly in the face of a hundred speculative questions, 'I do not know.' " (*Gospel Doctrine,* p. 9.) And yet our focus need not be upon the unknown; rather, we can emphasize what we do know. This is the pattern found in scripture, the pattern whereby a prophet says, in essence, "I don't know this, but let me tell you what I do know." An angel asked Nephi: "Knowest thou the condescension of God?" Now note the young prophet's response: "I know that he loveth his children; nevertheless, I do not know the meaning of all things." (1 Nephi 11:16–17.) Alma, in discoursing on the coming of the Messiah to the people of Gideon, said: "Behold, I do not say that he will come among us at the time of his dwelling in his mortal tabernacle; for behold, the Spirit hath not said unto me that this should be the case. *Now as to this thing I do not know; but this much I do know,* that the Lord God hath power to do all things which are according to his word." (Alma 7:8; italics added.) Later in the Nephite story, Alma, in counseling his errant son Corianton, spoke concerning life after death. He indicated that he did not know the particulars, the details concerning the time of the resurrection. "There is a time appointed unto men that they shall rise from the dead; and there is a space between the time of death and the resurrection. And now, concerning this space of time, what becometh of the souls of men is the thing which I have inquired diligently of the Lord to know; and *this is the thing of which I do know.*" (Alma 40:8–9; italics added.)

Though it may be obvious at this point, one cannot be lazy or lethargic in one's quest to find answers to difficult questions. There is an effort required in the spiritual realm, at least as extensive an effort as that associated with finding solutions in the world of physical phenomena. "It is a paradox," Elder John A. Widtsoe noted, "that men will gladly devote time every day for many years to learn a science or an art; yet will expect to win a knowledge of the gospel, which comprehends all sciences and arts, through perfunctory glances at books or occasional listening to sermons. The gospel should be studied more intensively," he stated, "than any school or college subject. They who pass opinion on the gospel without having given it intimate and careful study are not lovers of truth, and their opinions are worthless." (*Evidences and Reconciliations,* pp. 16–17.) It is one thing to know that the gospel is true, and another to know the gospel. And we certainly cannot expect to understand some of the more difficult doctrinal matters, for example, save we pay the price in appropriate study and investigation.

It is one thing to be ignorant of a matter. It is quite another to allow that ignorance to be transformed into a type of festering spiritual sore that robs one of peace and shakes the foundations of one's faith. Though the following quotation is rather lengthy, I feel it is an excellent statement on the matter of doubt. Elder Widtsoe explained: "Doubt usually means uncertainty. You doubt the presence of gold in the ore, though there are yellow flakes in it; or that the man is a thief, though stolen goods are found in his possession; or that a principle of the gospel is correctly interpreted by the speaker. What you really mean is that the evidence in your possession is insufficient to convince you that there is gold in the ore, or that the man is a thief, or that the gospel principle has been explained correctly. Doubt arises from lack of evidence.

"Intelligent people cannot long endure such doubt. It must be resolved. Proof must be secured of the presence of gold in the ore, or of the dishonesty of the man, or of the correctness of the doctrinal exposition. Consequently, we set about to remove doubt by gathering information and making tests concerning the subject in question. Doubt, then, becomes converted into inquiry or investigation.

"After proper inquiries, using all the powers at our command, the truth concerning the subject becomes known, or it remains unknown to be unravelled perhaps at some future time. The weight of evidence is on one side or the other. Doubt is removed. Doubt, therefore, can be and should be only a temporary condition. Certainly, a question cannot forever be suspended between heaven and earth; it is either answered or unanswered. As the results of an inquiry appear, doubt must flee. . . .

"The strong man is not afraid to say, 'I do not know'; the

weak man simpers and answers, 'I doubt.' Doubt, unless transmuted into inquiry, has no value or worth in the world. Of itself it has never lifted a brick, driven a nail, or turned a furrow. To take pride in being a doubter, without earnestly seeking to remove the doubt, is to reveal shallowness of thought and purpose. . . .

"Doubt of the right kind—that is, honest questioning— leads to faith. Such doubt impels men to inquiry which always opens the door to truth. The scientist in his laboratory, the explorer in distant parts, the prayerful man upon his knees— these and all inquirers like them find truth. They learn that some things are known, others are not. They cease to doubt. They settle down with the knowledge they possess to make the forces of nature do their bidding, knowing well that they will be victorious; and that more knowledge will come to them, if sought, to yield new power.

"On the other hand, the stagnant doubter, one content with himself, unwilling to make the effort, to pay the price of discovery, inevitably reaches unbelief and miry darkness. His doubts grow like poisonous mushrooms in the dim shadows of his mental and spiritual chambers. At last, blind like the mole in his burrow, he usually substitutes ridicule for reason, and indolence for labor. The simplest truth is worth the sum of all such doubts. He joins the unhappy army of doubters who, weakened by their doubts, have at all periods of human history allowed others, men of faith, to move the world into increasing light." (*Evidences and Reconciliations,* pp. 31–32.)

There are many things we will need to wait on, many questions we will encounter whose answers will definitely not be forthcoming right away. Some things we need to be willing to "put on a shelf." We continue our searching, our prayer, our discussions, but we wait patiently upon the Lord. I, like many others, do not understand for the present all the things that took place in the history of our Church or all the doctrines preached by leaders of the Church. But my confidence and my trust in Joseph Smith and his successors is implicit. We simply do not have the whole story yet. Joseph and Brigham and John and Wilford are not here to fill in the gaps in our knowledge, nor are the rank and file members of the Church from bygone days available for oral interviews and clarifications. We must do all that we can in the present to reconstruct the past, to write and understand the story of the Latter-day Saints, but we must be patient, avoiding the temptation to attribute improper motivation or to jump prematurely to conclusions; we need to give the leaders of the Church the benefit of the doubt. The Lord will vindicate the words and works of his anointed servants in time. Of that I have no doubt. In the meantime, we must receive their words, as the revelation declares, "in all patience and faith." (D&C 21:5.)

While serving as missionaries in the eastern states, my senior companion and I entered a town in New Jersey and began a systematic program of door-to-door contacting. We had not worked in the area for long before it became obvious that the local Protestant ministers had prepared their parishioners for our coming. At almost every door we were greeted with, "Oh, you must be the Mormons. Here, we have something for you." They then handed us an anti-Mormon tract. We collected hundreds of these pamphlets and stacked them in the corner of our apartment. Curiosity eventually got the better of us, and both of us decided to peruse some of the material. There were many things we read that were disturbing, but I remember most of all an issue regarding the

LDS view of the Godhead that caused me extreme uneasiness. My companion was no less disturbed than I. Day after day we went about our task of knocking on doors, being rejected and rebuffed, and expanding our collection of anti-Mormon propaganda. When I had reached the point of spiritual discomfort where I couldn't stand the tension any longer, I said to my companion at lunch, "Elder Henderson, what if the Church isn't true?" I expected him to be startled by such a question. He was not. He responded, "I've been wondering the same thing."

Now I was startled. He was my senior companion, my leader, my example. "What if the Baptist church is right?" I asked. "What if the Catholics have had priesthood authority all along?" "I don't know what to say," he replied. It was a depressing time for both of us.

I can still remember how very intense and focused my prayers were during those difficult days. I pleaded with God to give me an answer, to give me a feeling, to give me something! I lifted my voice heavenward constantly—on my knees whenever I had occasion and in my heart all through the day. For more than two weeks we struggled. I had concluded—though I had not expressed this thought to my companion—that unless some resolution to my soul-searching came soon, I would go home. I felt then that I just couldn't be a hypocrite, that I couldn't bear testimony of something I didn't know was true. (If I had only understood the principle that a testimony is strengthened through the bearing of it, I could have gone on.) The questions I had about the Godhead were eating me alive. I was confused, ashamed, and terribly uncomfortable. One afternoon when we returned home for lunch, I sat in the easy chair in the small living room in the apartment. I propped my feet up, sat back, let out a sigh, and for some reason picked up a copy of the pamphlet "Joseph Smith Tells His Own Story." I opened the brochure and began reading. I was not five lines into the Prophet's opening statement before I was absolutely wrapped in a feeling of warmth and comfort that I had never known, almost as though someone had covered me with a type of spiritual blanket. Though I heard no words, the feelings that came to me seemed to say, "Of course this work is true. You know it is true. And now, as to your question, be patient. You'll understand soon enough." This was all I needed for the time being. It was inspiration. It was perspective. I shared my newfound faith with Elder Henderson, he felt a similar spirit of comfort, and we went about our task with more courage in our conviction. The difficult matter had been put on a shelf. The answer to my question, by the way, did come in time. Within a year I was blessed with a companion who understood thoroughly the issue and helped me to see an aspect of the gospel that to me had previously been a mystery.

I do not hesitate to acknowledge that I have placed many things on a shelf over the past twenty years. A number of those items have come down from the shelf as information and inspiration have brought light and understanding where darkness and uncertainty had been. Some matters will probably stay on the shelf until that glorious millennial day when the God of heaven makes known those things "which have passed, and hidden things which no man knew, things of the earth, by which it was made, and the purpose and the end thereof—things most precious, things that are above, and things that are beneath, things that are in the earth, and upon the earth, and in heaven." (D&C 101:32–34.)

There is a final suggestion that we might consider with respect to finding answers to difficult questions. It is a bit more painful and requires a strict honesty on our part, a willingness to reflect and introspect. "Search your hearts," was Joseph Smith's challenge and invitation, "and see if you are like God. I have searched mine," he added, "and feel to repent of all my sins." (*Teachings of the Prophet Joseph Smith,* p. 216.) Some things are kept from us because we are not prepared, not spiritually ready, to receive them. Some things we cannot comprehend because our souls are not attuned to the Infinite, because we are in sin. Sometimes our wilful submission to sin points up our unbelief, and unbelief frequently leads to misunderstanding or lack of understanding. (See Mosiah 26:1–3.) There is an incident in the Book of Mormon that symbolizes our dilemma and at the same time prescribes a means of recovery. Nephi and Lehi, sons of Helaman, taught the gospel to the Lamanites with great power and persuasion. A multitude of people watched with much interest as Nephi and Lehi, held as prisoners up to this time, were "encircled about as if by fire." The earth shook, a cloud of darkness overshadowed the people, and "an awful solemn fear came upon them." A voice was heard: "Repent ye, repent ye, and seek no more to destroy my servants whom I have sent unto you to declare good tidings." This voice was heard three times. Aminadab, a Nephite by birth, sensed what needed to be done to dispel the darkness. Now note: *"You must repent,* and cry unto the voice, even until ye shall have faith in Christ . . . ; *and when ye shall do this, the cloud of darkness shall be removed from overshadowing you."* (Helaman 5:21–41; italics added.) And so it is with each of us. As we call on the Lord in secret and solemn prayer, express to him our willingness to forsake our sins and follow his Son in truth and righteousness, and live in such a manner thereafter that we evidence the sincerity of our covenant, we will once again walk in the light. The film of facade, the dimming and damning influences of duplicity and double-mindedness, and the painful and poignant pull of pride will have been removed. It will be as if a cloud of spiritual darkness has been blown away by the winds of faith and trust in our Redeemer. We then can begin to see things as they really are. We can be at peace.

Chapter Two

Pursuing a Sane and Balanced Course

One sign of our spiritual maturity is steadiness, our capacity to navigate the strait and narrow path in a stable and fairly consistent manner, to work with zeal but patient maturity, to stay in the mainstream of the Church. God does not expect us to work ourselves into spiritual, emotional, or physical oblivion, nor does he desire that the members of the true Church be truer than true. There is little virtue in excess, even in gospel excess. In fact, as members of the Church exceed the bounds of propriety and go beyond the established mark, they open themselves to deception and ultimately to destruction. Imbalance leads to instability. If Satan cannot cause us to lie or steal or smoke or be immoral, it just may be that he will cause our strength—our zeal for goodness and righteousness—to become our weakness. He will encourage excess, for surely any virtue, when taken to the extreme, becomes a vice.

Excessive Zeal and Gospel Hobbies

A friend of mine shared the following experience. More than forty years ago he and his wife became acquainted with an older couple in their ward. This couple were about as devoted to the Church as people could be. The wife had been raised in the Church; her husband had come in contact with the missionaries and been baptized while in the military. Like most of us, this couple had had their ups and downs in the faith, had struggled with a commandment here and there, but had managed to put much of the foolishness of youth behind them. In their eagerness to "make up" for all the times they may have disappointed the Lord, they determined upon a course to do everything they could to live the laws of the gospel with perfectness. They would leave no stone unturned, no *i* undotted. If the Lord through his Church asked for 10 percent of their income as a tithing, they would pay 15 percent. If Church members were asked to fast once per month, they would fast once per week. If most people studied the scriptures an hour per day, they would search and ponder and pray over holy writ for two hours. And so on and so on.

My friend mentioned one other aspect of this couple's zeal—their observance of the Word of Wisdom. Not only did they abstain from alcohol, tobacco, tea, coffee, and harmful drugs but they also felt it was important to avoid white bread and chocolate. They insisted that their children also follow such a course, which brought no end to frustration and contention in their home. What had in the beginning been merely a simple effort to demonstrate their willingness to keep all the commandments became, in time, an arduous task, a burdensome and uncomfortable labor. Resentment grew in the hearts of the children. Neighbors felt uncomfortable around them. In observing the Word of Wisdom, what had begun as a matter of health became a matter of "religious" fanaticism; the children (and the neighbors) were taught to avoid chocolate with at least as much enthusiasm as the Saints had been taught to avoid sexual immorality. Subtle suggestions to comply with this "higher law" were soon transformed into divine directives. Persons who chose to observe the commandments in a more traditional way were viewed as lacking in valor. The couple withdrew into themselves and away from others who did not share their zeal. It was only a matter of time before Satan capitalized on their imbalance and led them to the brink of spiritual destruction. Only through the love, patience, and vigilance of priesthood leaders, loved ones, and friends were they delivered from their error and enabled to begin the slow and painful return to the true strait and narrow path.

We all know that we would be better off physically if we avoided chocolate, or at least if we ate it in moderation. But that is not the issue. In this case, and in too many others, persons who determine upon a course which will take them beyond the expected, above the required, inevitably begin to expect the same of others. It becomes a "religious" principle, one to which persons are proselyted. The overzealous tend to judge others by their own standard. I have known persons who are so completely committed to family history and temple work that they constantly badger and criticize others who are not in a position to do as much as they are doing. Obviously such work is a vital part of our ministry as Latter-day Saints; we neglect it at the peril of our eternal salvation. I also know, as Elder Dallin H. Oaks has pointed out, that there is a time and a season for all things, that individuals' specific contributions to the kingdom are and must be private consecrations between the persons and God. That is why the leaders of the Church have discouraged quotas and pre-established goals for temple work. "Our efforts to promote temple and family history work," Elder Oaks has noted, "should be such as to accomplish the work of the Lord, not to impose guilt on his children. Members of this church have many individual cir-cumstances — age, health, education, place of residence, fam-ily responsibilities, financial circumstances, accessibility to sources for individual or library research, and many others. If we encourage members in this work without taking these individual circumstances into account, we may do more to impose guilt than to further the work. . . .

"There are many different things our members can do to help in the redeeming of the dead, in temple and family history work. Some involve callings. Others are personal. All are expressions of devotion and discipleship. All present op-portunities for sacrifice and service." (*Ensign,* June 1989, pp. 6–7.)

One could take a simple observance such as fasting or praying and soon find, with just the slightest amount of extra zeal, that these wonderful principles, given for the blessing and benefit of mankind, contribute to error. I spoke once to a temple president who described what had happened over the years in the temple in which he and his wife had served. He said that there was a particular room set aside as a prayer room, a place where patrons of the temple could retire for pondering and meditation, where they could go to seek in-spiration or guidance on personal matters. For a long time, he said, the room served a useful purpose: it reminded the patrons that temples were places of learning and revelation, holy edifices where we go to attend to sacred matters for the living as well as for the dead. In time, however, the room became such a popular spot that long lines often wound their way around the celestial room, where hosts of people stood waiting their turn.

What we are describing here is a phenomenon known as

"gospel hobbies" — the tendency to take a good thing and run it into the ground. We are speaking of the evils of excess, even in noble and worthwhile causes. Gospel hobbies lead to imbalance. To instability. To distraction. To misperception. They are dangerous and should be avoided as we would any other sin. President Joseph F. Smith said: "We frequently look about us and see people who incline to extremes, who are fanatical. We may be sure that this class of people do not understand the gospel. They have forgotten, if they ever knew, that it is very unwise to take a fragment of truth and treat it as if it were the whole thing." (*Gospel Doctrine*, p. 122.) To ride a gospel hobby is to participate in and perpetuate fanaticism. Harsh words, but true ones. On another occasion President Smith taught: "Brethren and sisters, don't have hobbies. Hobbies are dangerous in the Church of Christ. They are dangerous because they give undue prominence to certain principles or ideas to the detriment and dwarfing of others just as important, just as binding, just as saving as the favored doctrines or commandments.

"Hobbies give to those who encourage them a false aspect of the gospel of the Redeemer; they distort and place out of harmony its principles and teachings. The point of view is unnatural. Every principle and practice revealed from God is essential to man's salvation, and to place any one of them unduly in front, hiding and dimming all others is unwise and dangerous; it jeopardizes our salvation, for it darkens our minds and beclouds our understandings. . . .

"We have noticed this difficulty: that Saints with hobbies are prone to judge and condemn their brethren and sisters who are not so zealous in the one particular direction of their pet theory as they are. . . . There is another phase of this difficulty — the man with a hobby is apt to assume an 'I am holier than thou' position, to feel puffed up and conceited, and to look with distrust, if with no severer feeling, on his brethren and sisters who do not so perfectly live that one particular law." (*Gospel Doctrine,* pp. 116–17.) In other words, an emphasis upon excellence in gospel living—as manifest in gospel hobbies—can result in pride, the father of all other sins. President Harold B. Lee reiterated counsel the First Presidency (Joseph F. Smith, Anthon H. Lund, and Charles W. Penrose) gave in 1913: "At . . . times people who pride themselves on their strict observance of the rules and ordinances and ceremonies of the Church are led astray by false spirits, who exercise an influence so imitative of that which proceeds from a Divine source that even these persons, who think they are the 'very elect,' find it difficult to discern the essential difference." (*Improvement Era,* June 1970, pp. 63–64.)

True excellence in gospel living—compliance with the established laws and ordinances in a quiet and patient manner—results in humility, in greater reliance upon God, and in a broadening love and acceptance of one's fellow man. There is a principle here: what I am doing in the name of goodness ought to bring me closer to those I love and serve, ought to turn my heart toward people, rather than causing me to turn my nose up in judgmental scorn and rejection. The greatest man to walk the earth, the only fully perfect human being, looked with tenderness and compassion upon those whose ways and actions were less than perfect. He is the Exemplar.

Elder Bruce R. McConkie has similarly written: "It is . . . my experience that people who ride gospel hobbies, who try to qualify themselves as experts in some specialized field, who try to make the whole plan of salvation revolve around some field of particular interest to them — it is my experience that such persons are usually spiritually immature and spiritually unstable. This includes those who devote themselves — as though by divine appointment — to setting forth the signs of the times; or, to expounding about the Second Coming; or, to a faddist interpretation of the Word of Wisdom; or, to a twisted emphasis on temple work or any other doctrine or practice. The Jews of Jesus' day made themselves hobbiests and extremists in the field of Sabbath observance, and it colored and blackened their whole way of worship. *We would do well to have a sane, rounded, and balanced approach to the whole gospel and all of its doctrines."* (*Doctrines of the Restoration,* p. 232; italics added.)

Not unrelated to excessive zeal and overmuch righteousness is the tendency by some to attempt to force spiritual things. What would we think of a father who said to his fourteen-year-old son: "Larry, if you really love me you will be tall. I have been short all my life. I love basketball and have always wanted to be a star forward on a successful team. But it's never worked out. If you love me, if you have any respect for me as your father, you will grow to be six foot eight." Strange, isn't it? In fact, such a request would be cruel and unkind, because Larry has little control over how tall he will be. He can eat the right foods, train and work out, and do everything within his power to be big and strong, but he cannot control how tall he will be. In a way, it's just the same with spiritual growth. We cannot program it. We cannot specify and delineate and produce. We cannot prepare formulae and plans that will result in specific spiritual phenomena. We cannot say with certitude that if one does X and Y and Z, a dream or vision will be forthcoming; that if one does A or B or C consistently, one will be able to prophesy or speak in tongues. We can prepare the soil, provide a setting for development, but that is all. We must exercise patience and trust in the Lord and his purposes.

I knew one man who claimed that he would be perfect by the age of thirty. He set out on a deliberate program, organized his goals according to a ten-year, five-year, one-year, monthly, weekly, and daily plan. He pushed and pulled and stretched and reached spiritually, as much as any person I have known. But he was not perfect at thirty. You cannot force spiritual things. I am acquainted with a woman who announced to several of our friends that she would make her calling and election sure by the time she was fifty years old. She has been faithful in the Church. She has long since passed the age of fifty and is terribly discouraged because the goal of her existence, so far as she knows, has not been realized. You cannot force spiritual things. Endless prayers, lengthy scripture vigils, excessive fasting—all of these, though at first well-intended, may come to be more a curse than a blessing. Gospel growth must come slowly, steadily, gradually. Elder Boyd K. Packer has warned: "Such words as *compel, coerce, constrain, pressure, demand* do not describe our privileges with the Spirit.

"You can no more force the Spirit to respond than you can force a bean to sprout, or an egg to hatch before its time. You can create a climate to foster growth; you can nourish, and protect; but you cannot force or compel: You must await the growth.

"Do not be impatient to gain great spiritual knowledge. Let it grow, help it grow; but do not force it, or you will open the way to be misled." (*"That All May Be Edified,"* p. 338; italics in original.)

For years I wrestled with the meaning of the parable of

the ten virgins, as recorded in Matthew 25. The scene seemed so wrong, the message so counter to all that the Master had taught. Why couldn't the wise virgins just share their oil? If each one just contributed a little, I reasoned, perhaps each one, or at least some, of the "foolish" ones could make it to the wedding to meet the Bridegroom. And then an experience taught me the answer to my query. While I was serving as a priesthood leader, a husband and wife came to see me. They were both distressed about the state of their marriage and family; things seemed to be coming apart in their lives. "How can I help?" I asked. "We need more spirituality in our home," the wife answered. I asked a few questions. "How often do you pray as a family?" They answered that their schedules precluded any kind of family prayer. "Have you been able to hold family home evening?" "Bill and I bowl on Monday nights," was the response. "Do you read the scriptures as a family or as individuals?" The answer from the husband: "Reading hurts my eyes." "Well, then, how can I help you?" Again the reply: "We want the Spirit in our lives."

It was as though they were saying to me, "Brother Millet, could you reach down into your heart and lend us five years of daily prayer, ten years of regular scripture study, and fifteen years of family spiritual activities?" I couldn't do it. I realized dramatically that there are some things that we simply cannot share. I also came to appreciate that like the small oil lamps of the Middle East, which require a careful and methodical and slow effort to fill, so in our own lives we need to build our reservoirs of faith and spiritual experience gradually and consistently. Consistent gospel growth—that was the answer. A colleague of mine drew my attention to these words of President Spencer W. Kimball: "The foolish asked the others to share their oil, but spiritual preparedness cannot be shared in an instant. . . . This was not selfishness or unkindness. The kind of oil that is needed to illuminate the way and light up the darkness is not shareable. . . . In our lives the oil of preparedness is accumulated drop by drop in righteous living." (*Faith Precedes the Miracle,* pp. 255–56.)

Finally, in our eagerness to prepare and do all that is required, we must be careful that our personal expectations, though rigorous, are realistic. Zion of old became a society of the pure in heart "in process of time" (Moses 7:21), and, with but few exceptions, members of the Church become Saints of the Most High in similar fashion. Except for a limited number of cases that are so miraculous they are written up in scripture, being born again is a process; we are born again gradually, from one level of spiritual grace to a higher. Almost always people are sanctified—made clean and holy and pure through the blood of Christ by the medium of the Holy Ghost—in gradual, line upon line fashion. Thus, ultimate perfection and salvation are processes. One great challenge we face in our quest for spiritual maturity is to balance a type of divine discontent, a constant yearning for improvement and growth, with what Nephi called a "perfect brightness of hope" (2 Nephi 31:20), the assurance born of the Spirit that although we are not perfect—we have much sanctification and perfection ahead of us—we have a hope in Christ, a quiet confidence that in and through him we shall in time overcome all things and go on to eternal life.

Mormon Gnosticism

The empire of Alexander the Great, as a political entity, did not long survive his death in 323 B.C., but the cultural empire he founded lasted for nearly one thousand years, until the rise of Islam and the Arab conquests in the seventh century after Christ. Greek or Hellenistic influence was profound—upon the Roman empire, upon the world of Judaism, and, unfortunately, upon the early Christian Church. As Zenos had declared in prophetic vision, the grafting of branches from the "wild olive tree" (Gentile influence) resulted in a season of strength for the Church. (See Jacob 5:17.) But it was only a matter of time before the doctrines of the prophets and the ideas of the philosophers came into conflict; those with eyes to see were aware that attempts to merge the revelations of the temple of God with the doctrines of Plato would be abortive to the true Christian faith. Ecumenism would lead to shared impotence. And so it did.

In the first few centuries of the Christian era there grew up a movement which came to be known as Gnosticism. The word *gnosis* connoted for them knowledge, not a general kind of knowledge but rather a special, saving knowledge. The Gnostics were a group who claimed to possess the esoteric teachings of Jesus, the supposedly sacred and secret messages reserved only for those who sought to rise above the mundane and liberate themselves from the fetters of ignorance and a confining physical world. They decried and defied, for the most part, what they believed to be a stifling and restrictive priesthood hierarchy of the orthodox church. Salvation was an individual experience, which came through spiritual illumination of the mysteries of godliness. Theirs was an emphasis upon the damning nature of this fallen world (and the physical body) and the supernal treasures to be had through transcending our condition here and ascending to pure spirit. Some of the Gnostics, known as Docetists (from a Greek word meaning "appears" or "seems") went so far as to claim that Jesus did not really come to earth with a corporeal body,

but—since the body was something to be shunned and overcome—it only appeared that he had a physical tabernacle.
(It is interesting, therefore, to consider the significance of
John's teachings in 1 John 4:1–3; 2 John 1:7.) We have heard
much over the years about the effect of Roman persecution
on the early Christian Church, but in reality the death knell
for Christianity came through hellenization—the mingling of
Greek philosophy with the scriptures and teachings of the
earliest Christian Church. In and through the perpetuation
of this hybrid heresy was lost the true knowledge of God, of
man, and of the purpose of life. The great apostasy followed.

In the times of restitution we have not been without our
own little Gnostic groups. There was Hiram Page, who sought
to reveal things about Zion (D&C 28); Mrs. Hubble, who
claimed to be receiving divine direction for the Saints (D&C
43); some who spoke of secret commissions and ordinations
under the hands of Joseph Smith; and others today who make
much of special callings or unusual insights. We have watched
with much interest and pain as a surprising number of the
Lord's people are lured away by voices that beckon for their
attention. Some charismatic figures boldly declare that only
those properly trained or credentialed can interpret scripture
or lead the way. Some speak openly of visions, dreams, or
revelations that entitle them to turn the Church in a direction
different from its present course. Frequently we hear from
some well-meaning Saints that we must reinstitute the united
order or bring back this idea or that practice. Where is our
safety? How can we know who to follow?

The prophets have been especially vocal in their warnings
against such movements. As we begin to mature in our citi-
zenship in the kingdom, we find ourselves less attracted to
such things, less enamored of the strange, the sensational, or

the exotic; rather, we become more prone to focus upon and delight in the fundamental principles and doctrines of the gospel, more prone to teach and act with simplicity, more prone to stress the things the Lord's servants stress. We take seriously the scriptural charge to say "none other things than that which the prophets and apostles have written, and that which is taught [us] by the Comforter through the prayer of faith." (D&C 52:9; see also v. 36.) We begin to realize that there are no secret doctrines, no private ways of life, nothing that the general authorities believe or practice that is not readily accessible to every member of the Church. Elder Boyd K. Packer spoke of the problem of claims to special ordination. "There have been too many names presented," he stated, "too many sustaining votes taken, too many ordinations and settings apart performed before too many witnesses; there have been too many records kept, too many certificates prepared, and too many pictures published in too many places for any one to be deceived as to who holds proper authority. Claims of special revelation or secret authority from the Lord or from the Brethren are false on the face of them and really utter nonsense!

"The Lord never operated that way; these things were not done in a corner (see Acts 26:26); there is light on every official call and every authorized ordination, and it has always been that way." (In Conference Report, Apr. 1985, p. 43.)

Safety and security in the midst of a babble of voices, even some voices from Latter-day Saints, are to be found in following the Brethren, in giving heed to the counsel and direction we receive from our leaders at the general conferences of the Church and in the official organs and publications of the Church. As members of the true church, we really ought to read and know and teach from the general conference addresses as much as we do from the standard works. I know from personal experience of the remarkable spiritual presence that accompanies our teaching and our presentations as we cite or quote the Brethren. We thus evidence our respect and appreciation for the words of the living oracles. When we are loyal to this principle, we would never seek to run before our leaders, to suggest that the Saints should do this or that when in fact those responsible for guiding the destiny of the Church and kingdom have not so spoken. President Joseph F. Smith observed that "no man possessing a correct understanding of the spirit of the gospel and of the authority and law of the Holy Priesthood will attempt for a moment to run before his file leader or to do anything that is not strictly in harmony with his wish and the authority that belongs to him. The moment a man in a subordinate position begins to usurp the authority of his leader, that moment he is out of his place, and proves by his conduct that he does not comprehend his duty, that he is not acting in the line of his calling, and is a dangerous character." (*Gospel Doctrine*, p. 185.)

A vital part of maturing in the faith is coming to acknowledge the position of those called to lead us, on both a general and a local level. Few people would go astray, would find themselves in apostasy or in the center of controversy, if they simply sought for and followed the counsel of their church leaders. People are not necessarily called to positions of responsibility because they are the most qualified, the most talented, or the most gifted gospel scholar. Our challenge is to sustain, that is, give our full loyalty and support, to people who are often less than perfect, even people whom we might feel to be less capable than ourselves. "Here is a lesson for all of us in this Church," President David O. McKay said.

"Let us . . . recognize the local authority. The bishop may be a humble man. Some of you may think you are superior to him, and you may be, but he is given authority direct from our Father in heaven. You recognize it. Seek his advice, the advice of your stake president. If they cannot answer your difficulties or your problems, they will write to the General Authorities and get the advice needed. Recognition of authority is an important principle." (In Conference Report, Oct. 1965, p. 105.)

Indeed, those who, through pride or an elevated sense of self-worth, ignore or reject the counsel of bishops or stake presidents will lose the Spirit of the Lord and be left to themselves. It is a small thing to take counsel from a local leader, but it is vital to our eternal welfare. In fact, as the scriptures attest, it is by small means that great things are brought to pass. (See 1 Nephi 16:29; Alma 37:6–7; D&C 64:33.) "You can put it down in your little black book," Elder Boyd K. Packer has taught, "that if you will not be loyal in the small things, you will not be loyal in the large things. If you will not respond to the so-called insignificant or menial tasks which need to be performed in the Church and Kingdom, there will be no opportunity for service in the so-called greater challenges. A man who says he will sustain the President of the Church or the General Authorities, but cannot sustain his own bishop, is deceiving himself. The man who will not sustain the bishop of his ward and the president of his stake will not sustain the President of the Church." (*Follow the Brethren*, pp. 4–5.) We must never forget that the organization of the Church—the officers and teachers and other helps—have been provided "for the perfecting of the saints, for the work of the ministry, for the edifying of the body of Christ"—meaning, of course, the members of the

Church. "Till we all come in the unity of the faith, and of the knowledge of the Son of God, unto a perfect [fully formed, mature] man, unto the measure of the stature of the fulness of Christ: *that we henceforth be no more children, tossed to and fro, and carried about with every wind of doctrine, by the sleight of men, and cunning craftiness, whereby they lie in wait to deceive;* but speaking the truth in love, may *grow up into him in all things, which is the head, even Christ.*" (Ephesians 4:11–15; italics added.)

There are ways of knowing the truth, of discerning the veracity and fruitfulness of a doctrine or a point of view. Joseph Smith pointed out that nothing is a greater injury to the children of men than to be under the influence of a false spirit when we suppose we have the Spirit of God. (*Teachings of the Prophet Joseph Smith,* p. 205.) If someone comes to us claiming a special appointment, special knowledge that is not available to most members, special training and abilities that entitle him or her to interpret scripture or clarify doctrine beyond what has been given by the authorized servants of God, we might ask the following:

1. *Is the person claiming a divine communication or insight acting within the bounds of his or her respective assignment?* The Lord's house is a house of order, not a house of confusion. (D&C 132:8.) Chaos would ensue rather quickly if every person could receive revelations for every other person in the Church, irrespective of stewardship. Joseph Smith the Prophet taught that it is contrary to the economy of God for people to receive revelation for those higher in authority than themselves. (*Teachings of the Prophet Joseph Smith,* p. 21.) He also explained that it is the "privilege of any officer in this Church to obtain revelations, so far as relates to his particular calling and duty in the Church." (*Teachings of the Prophet*

Joseph Smith, p. 111.) Through the generations people have repeatedly insisted that they have received direction for the Church regarding its financial status, its placement of temples, its meetings or schedule, and its doctrinal positions on this or that topic. No matter the genuineness or sincerity of the supposed recipients, the directives are not of God. The Lord simply does not work that way. There is order. There are proper channels.

2. *Is the recipient of the communication worthy to receive the same?* Though we may not always be in a position to judge another's worthiness, we are generally pretty good judges of our own. The revelations indicate that the works of God are brought to pass through those who are clean, who have been purified from the sins of the world. (See 3 Nephi 8:1; D&C 50:28.) If I have received what I believe to be a revelation from God, then it is perfectly appropriate for me to ask (and it would be well if I asked with sincerity and humility) whether I was in spiritual condition to receive such a matter from God. While I was serving as a priesthood leader several years ago, a young man came to visit with me on numerous occasions about what he believed to be revelations from God. He told me of visions and angelic appearances, of specific messages about his life. Such would be well within the bounds of propriety, except for one thing: the young man was also guilty of gross violations of the law of chastity, so much so that his membership was at stake. Without being cruel or unkind, allowing that no one of us is perfect, we must attend to the principle that God will not work through polluted channels. In fact, President Harold B. Lee pointed out: "We get our answers from the source of the power we list to obey. If we're following the ways of the devil, we'll get answers from

the devil. If we're keeping the commandments of God, we'll get our answers from God." (*Stand Ye in Holy Places,* p. 138.)

3. *Is the communication in harmony with the teachings in the standard works and those of the living prophets?* When people claim to have received word that they should join a polygamous cult or participate in a demonic practice or be disloyal or disobedient to the government, one wonders how they can justify their position. When others indicate that they have been directed by the Lord to lie or cheat or steal or be immoral, one wonders how such actions can square with the teachings of the Church. Often individuals claim that their case is an exception to the rule. We would do well as a people to stay within the rules and avoid the exceptions, especially when such exceptions violate the law and order of the kingdom of God. Those still convinced that what they are commanded to do is of God would then do well to counsel with their priesthood leaders and then follow that counsel emphatically. On the other hand, certain groups of people contend that the Church should be doing this or that, so as to be in harmony with such and such a scripture. We need only remind ourselves that ours is a living constitution, a living church (D&C 1:30), and that the principle on which the government of heaven is conducted is, as Joseph Smith testified, "revelation adapted to the circumstances in which the children of the kingdom are placed." (*Teachings of the Prophet Joseph Smith,* p. 256.) Wise counsel for the Saints was given by Elder Bruce R. McConkie when he said: "The proper course for all of us is to stay in the mainstream of the Church. This is the Lord's Church, and it is led by the spirit of inspiration, and *the practice of the Church constitutes the interpretation of the scripture.*" (*Doctrines of the Restoration,* p. 66; italics added.)

4. *Does the communication edify or instruct? Is it consistent with the dignity that should attend something that comes from the Almighty?* While I was teaching seminary many years ago, I spoke often to the students of the need to remain open to the Spirit and to be prepared to receive its quiet promptings. After class one day a young lady asked if she could visit with me. She explained that on the previous night she had had a wonderful experience that she wanted to share. Not knowing the nature of the experience, I invited her to proceed. She said that her parents had left her alone at home for the evening while they went to dinner. She was sitting in the living room listening to music when, she indicated, the Spirit came upon her and said: "Get up. Run into your room." She did so. The voice then said: "Get under the bed," which she did. It then said: "Get out from under the bed and run outside into the backyard," which she did. Then: "Hide behind the wood pile." She explained that she stayed behind the wood pile for a while, until she was ordered around, back and forth, from one place to another in her family's rather large backyard. This lasted for about half an hour. The young woman turned to me and with much emotion said: "Isn't it wonderful how the Spirit can work with us?" I smiled and nodded. I am in no position to judge whether her experience was genuine or not; perhaps there was some reason why the Lord would have a fifteen-year-old rushing about at eight o'clock at night in the backyard. But I doubt it. I rather suppose that she was responding to whatever thought came into her mind that evening. The Prophet taught that God's revelations communicate something of worth to us. He also pointed out that a certain dignity and decorum are associated with divine communications. (See *Teachings of the Prophet Joseph Smith,* pp. 203–4, 209.)

5. *Does the communication build our faith and strengthen our commitment?* There is a litmus test that can be applied, a vital criterion that must be met if a supposed revelation is from God. We ask such questions as the following: Does this communication build my faith in Joseph Smith and the Restoration? Do I feel more motivated to serve faithfully in the Church and kingdom? Do I have confidence in the Lord's anointed servants today and in the destiny of the Church? God does not and will not work against himself; he will not confuse his people by having them believe or do things that would in any way weaken their hold on the iron rod. Those who suggest that the present Church is not progressive enough, that it needs to move faster toward this or that social or political or moral trend, act outside the bounds of propriety. They are walking on shaky ground. Joseph Smith stated: "That man who rises up to condemn others, finding fault with the Church, saying that they are out of the way, while he himself is righteous, then know assuredly, that that man is in the high road to apostasy; and if he does not repent, will apostatize, as God lives." (*Teachings of the Prophet Joseph Smith,* pp. 156–57.)

Principles That Preserve

The scriptures set forth certain principles that, if we are sensitive to their implications, will keep us on course and thus assist us in our quest for spiritual maturity. In his response to Satan's temptation to use divine powers for personal gain, the Savior answered: "It is written, Man shall not live by bread alone, but by every word that proceedeth out of the mouth of God." (Matthew 4:4; compare D&C 84:44.) *Every* word. Not every other word, not those words that are most acceptable and pleasing, not those words that support my own peculiar predispositions. Every word. Members of the Church would seldom become embroiled in doctrinal disputes, controversial dialogues, or gospel hobbies if they truly sought to live by every word that has come from the Lord, the scriptures, and the servants of God. To live by every word of God also implies the need to read and study widely, to be seeking for at least as much breadth in our gospel scholarship as we have depth, to seek to have the big picture. It has been wisely said that the greatest commentary on the scriptures is the scriptures themselves.

In preaching to the American Hebrews, the resurrected Lord delivered the doctrine of Christ, the need for all men and women to have faith, repent, be reborn, and endure faithfully to the end. He then declared: "Verily, verily, I say unto you, that this is my doctrine, and whoso buildeth upon this buildeth upon my rock, and the gates of hell shall not prevail against them. And *whoso shall declare more or less than this, and establish it for my doctrine, the same cometh of evil, and is not built upon my rock; but he buildeth upon a sandy foundation,* and the gates of hell stand open to receive such when the floods come and the winds beat upon them." (3 Nephi 11:39–40; italics added.) In a modern revelation, the Lord spoke of bringing forth the Book of Mormon, another testament of Jesus Christ, in order that he might establish his gospel to put down contention and disputation. "Behold, this is my doctrine—whosoever repenteth and cometh unto me, the same is my church. *Whosoever declareth more or less than this, the same is not of me, but is against me;* therefore he is not of my church." (D&C 10:62–68; italics added.) We need to live the gospel in such a way that we seek neither to add to nor take away from that which comes by and through the appointed channels of revelation for the Church.

This principle is not unrelated to the indictment sounded by Jacob against the ancient Jews. "The Jews were a stiff-necked people," he stated, "and *they despised the words of plainness,* and killed the prophets, and *sought for things that they could not understand.* Wherefore, because of their blindness, *which blindness came by looking beyond the mark,* they must needs fall; for God hath taken away his plainness from them, and delivered unto them many things which they cannot understand, because they desired it. And because they desired it God hath done it, that they may stumble." (Jacob 4:14; italics added.) What a fascinating situation! A people despised, or perhaps spurned or little appreciated, the words of plainness. They sought for things that they could not understand, perhaps meaning that they pushed themselves well beyond what had been revealed and thus beyond what men and women could appropriately grasp. They became blind by "looking beyond the mark." That is, they missed the point! They missed the main message! In the case of the Jews, they looked beyond the mark when Christ was the mark. They focused on the minutiae of the commentary concerning the law of Moses, when Christ was the message of the law. They confused means with ends, tokens with covenants, ritual with religion.

Elder Dean L. Larsen offered the following insights into this unusual scriptural passage from the Book of Mormon: "Jacob speaks of people who placed themselves in serious jeopardy in spiritual things because they were unwilling to accept simple, basic principles of truth. They entertained and intrigued themselves with 'things that they could not understand' (Jacob 4:14). They were apparently afflicted with a pseudosophistication and a snobbishness that gave them a false sense of superiority over those who came among them with the Lord's words of plainness. They went beyond the mark of wisdom and prudence, and obviously failed to stay within the circle of fundamental gospel truths, which provide a basis for faith. They must have reveled in speculative and theoretical matters that obscured for them the fundamental spiritual truths." (In Conference Report, Oct. 1987, p. 12.) We begin the process of spiritual maturity as we come to treasure up the word of the Lord, a sure means of avoiding deception (Joseph Smith–Matthew 1:37); as we find satisfaction and great delight in poring over and discussing the fundamental doctrines of the gospel; and as we wait upon the Lord to make us into new creatures and to reveal his purposes, all in his own time, and in his own way, and according to his own will. (See D&C 88:67–68.)

In summary, this is the Lord's church; he is at the helm. Revelation for the guidance of the Church as a whole will come through the ministry of those called as prophets, seers, and revelators. (See D&C 21:4–6; 28:2; 43:3–6; 90:3–5.) If it were the church of a man, then perhaps we might be justified in fretting and stewing over the status or the direction of the Church. But it is in good hands. Though individuals will lose the Spirit and fall away, there will never again be an apostasy of the Church. In 1905 the First Presidency — Joseph F. Smith, John R. Winder, and Anthon H. Lund — issued a statement entitled "One Mighty and Strong." Let me conclude things in this chapter by quoting a portion of the final two paragraphs of this important document:

"In conclusion, we would say that the Latter-day Saints by this time, should be so well settled in the conviction that God has established his Church in the earth for the last time, to remain, and no more to be thrown down, or destroyed; and that God's house is a house of order, of law, of regularity, that erratic disturbers of that order of men of restless temperament, who, through ignorance and egotism become vain babblers, yet make great pretensions to prophetic powers and other spiritual graces and gifts, ought not to have any influence with them, nor ought the Saints to be disturbed in their spirit by such characters and their theories. The Church of Christ is with the Saints. It has committed to it the law of God for its own government and perpetuation. It possesses every means for the correction of every wrong or abuse or error which may from time to time arise, and that without anarchy, or even revolution; it can do it by processes of evolution — by development, by an increase of knowledge, wisdom, patience and charity.

"The presiding quorums of the Church will always be composed of such men, they will be chosen in such manner, that the Saints can be assured that solid wisdom, righteousness, and conscientious adherence to duty, will characterize the policy of those who are entrusted with the administration of the affairs of the Church." (*Messages of the First Presidency,* 4:120.)

Chapter Three

Bearing Pure Testimony

We are engaged in the work of the Lord. This is his church. It administers his gospel and teaches his doctrine. It bears his priesthood and performs his ordinances. These are facts. They are true. A knowledge of such things, an inner certitude, we call a testimony. We cannot long progress in the kingdom without a witness of this work, without a testimony. It is a testimony of the Savior, of his gospel, and of the Restoration, that must be at the foundation of all we do. In fact, a knowledge of such things motivates us and impels us to faithfulness in the face of opposition; such an assurance helps us know why we do what we do.

A testimony is fundamental to our spiritual maturity. It is absolutely necessary to our spiritual preservation in a world whose discordant voices beckon us to loosen our hold on the rod of iron. President Heber C. Kimball issued a prophetic warning which should lead to sober thinking among Latter-day Saints: "We think we are secure here in the chambers of the everlasting hills," he said, "where we can close those few doors of the canyons against mobs and persecutors, the wicked and the vile, who have always beset us with violence and robbery, but I want to say to you, my brethren, the time is coming when we will be mixed up in these now peaceful valleys to that extent that it will be difficult to tell the face of a Saint from the face of an enemy to the people of God. Then, brethren, look out for the great sieve, for there will be a great sifting time, and many will fall; for I say unto you there is a *test,* a TEST, a TEST coming, and who will be able to stand? . . .

"Let me say to you, that many of you will see the time when you will have all the trouble, trial and persecution that you can stand, and plenty of opportunities to show that you are true to God and his work. This Church has before it many close places through which it will have to pass before the work of God is crowned with victory. To meet the difficulties that are coming, it will be necessary for you to have a knowledge of the truth of this work for yourselves. The difficulties will be of such a character that the man or woman who does not possess this personal knowledge or witness will fall. If you have not got the testimony, live right and call upon the Lord and cease not till you obtain it. If you do not you will not stand.

"Remember these sayings, for many of you will live to see them fulfilled. *The time will come when no man nor woman will be able to endure on borrowed light. Each will have to be guided by the light within himself. If you do not have it, how can you stand?*" (Orson F. Whitney, *Life of Heber C. Kimball,* pp. 446, 449–50; italics added.)

Acquiring the Witness

To *bear* a testimony has at least two meanings. It means, first of all, to possess one, in the sense that a person bears his armor or his priesthood. Second, it means to express or convey or declare it to others. It is true that it generally takes months and years and decades to develop the kind of spiritual conviction that proves to be the anchor to life and the safeguard against the trials spoken of by President Heber C. Kimball. On the other hand, there are some things we have always known. Many things that we come to know here we knew clearly in our premortal existence, before we came here. Thus the recognition of truth, the awareness of a verity, the sensitivity to significant doctrines—such things are, as President Joseph F. Smith taught so powerfully, "but the awakening of the memories of the spirit. Can we know anything here that we did not know before we came? Are not the means of knowledge in the first estate equal to those of this?" (*Gospel Doctrine,* p. 13.) As my colleague Joseph F. McConkie and I have written elsewhere: "We traditionally describe those who are born outside the Church and who subsequently join it as *converts,* implying that they turned from another belief to embrace the testimony of the Restoration. In fact, this is rarely the case. In most instances, those who have joined the Church tell us: 'There was no conversion. Everything the missionaries told me I already believed!' That which we call conversion may more aptly be described as an awakening, a distant memory, or an echo from the past. 'People ask me why I left my old church,' the so-called convert said. 'I tell them it was not a matter of my leaving my old church, but rather a matter of my coming home.' " (*The Holy Ghost,* p. 45.)

Though it is a bit tangential, let me relate an experience that teaches that all people—member and nonmember alike—are entitled to the Light of Christ, or, stated another way, the personal testimony of right and wrong. Many years ago I was asked to work with a woman who was reported to be having some serious psychological problems. I learned in my first visit with her that she had been raised in the Jewish faith, that for many years she was serious about her beliefs, a kind of devoted Reformed Jew. It took about two or three visits to get to the heart of the matter. She admitted to having been unfaithful to her husband and essentially was insisting that I assist her to feel more comfortable with her infidelity. I indicated that I could not. She said: "Why not? I'm paying you to help me!" I answered that I simply could not help anyone by asking that they go against their sense of values, their inner sense of right and wrong. She responded: "Oh no, you don't understand. I'm no longer a religious person. I'm no longer a practicing Jew. I don't believe anymore." I responded that this matter had nothing to do with religion. It had everything to do with being true to ourselves. She looked puzzled.

"You have been untrue to yourself," I said. "You know it, and there's no way to escape from that reality." "I tell you that I'm not religious anymore," she responded. "I don't have all those religious hang-ups I once had." I spent the next hour or so trying to help her get in touch with her own feelings, to hearken to the light within her. Finally I asked: "What are you feeling deep down, in your heart of hearts?" She paused a very long time and then replied: "I know I have done wrong. It's wrong, wrong, wrong! Help me do what's right." She knew, not just because she had been taught by men and women in this life, but because she had been taught by the Light of Christ within. I came away from that experience with an appreciation for the fact that all persons are entitled to know things, sweet and sacred things, and that they mature in spiritual things as they give heed to the light they already have.

Spiritual things are known. They are *known*. We need not

apologize for things we know by the power of the Spirit, for they are as real (if not more so) than the things we perceive in the physical world by means of the five senses. While I served as a bishop, I came to know and love the man who was my executive secretary. He and his family had joined the Church just a few years earlier. They were great people. My friend would stand in every testimony meeting and, without fail, say something like this: "I want to bear testimony that I . . . (long pause) . . . *believe* that this is the true Church. I want to say also that I really do . . . (pause) . . . *believe* that Joseph Smith is a prophet and that the Church is divinely led today." I listened month after month to his testimony. It was a sweet and touching expression. When I knew him quite well, and when the moment was right, I asked, "Larry, when you bear your testimony, why don't you just break down and say 'I *know*'?" He turned to me and gave me a strange look. "I couldn't do that," he responded, "because I haven't seen God. I wasn't personally present in the Sacred Grove in 1820. I'm not in the council meetings of the leadership of the Church today. I just can't say I *know*, because that wouldn't be true. For now I have to say that I *believe*."

We had a long and very productive chat. I showed him from scripture that spiritual things are known, not because they are seen with our physical eyes or felt with our hands or even heard with our ears, but because they are seen and felt and experienced with eyes and ears of faith. Indeed, believing is seeing. As Elder Boyd K. Packer has explained: "These delicate, refined spiritual communications are not seen with our eyes nor heard with our ears. And even though it is described as a voice, it is a voice that one feels more than one hears." (*"That All May Be Edified,"* p. 335.) I explained to Larry that spiritual realities make their way into our consciousness and our memory and our view of life in quiet but certain ways. They may be spiritual, but they are real. "O then, is not this real?" Alma asked concerning the beginnings of testimony. "I say unto you, Yea, because it is light; and whatsoever is light, is good, because it is discernible." (Alma 32:35.) Alma had seen angels. He had seen the Lord. But his testimony had come in softer, quieter, less dramatic ways (just as ours does). "Do ye not suppose that *I know* of these things [of Christ and his gospel] myself [that is, above and beyond what his prophetic predecessors had affirmed]? . . . Behold, I say unto you they are made known unto me by the Holy Spirit of God. Behold, I have fasted and prayed many days that I might *know* these things of myself. And now *I do know* of myself that they are true; for *the Lord God hath made them manifest unto me by his Holy Spirit;* and this is the spirit of revelation which is in me." (Alma 5:45–46; italics added.) *"I know with a witness that is more powerful than sight,"* President Harold B. Lee said to Brigham Young University students just three months before his death. "Sometime, if the spirit prompts me, I may feel free to tell you more, but may I say to you that *I know as though I had seen,* that He lives, that He is real, that God the Father and his Son are living realities, personalities with bodies, parts, and passions—glorified beings. If you believe that, then you are safe. If you don't believe it, then struggle for that witness, and all will be well with you." ("Be Loyal to the Royal within You," *Brigham Young University Speeches of the Year, 1973,* p. 103; italics added.)

Paul taught that faith comes through hearing the word of God. (See Romans 10:17.) Joseph Smith added: "Faith comes by hearing the word of God, through the testimony of the servants of God; that testimony is always attended by the

Spirit of prophecy and revelation." (*Teachings of the Prophet Joseph Smith,* p. 148.) We begin with the Light of Christ within us, which quietly points out right from wrong and which assists us in discerning the ways of the Lord from the ways of the world. Our faith and our testimony then begin to grow as we hear the gospel declared by one who knows, by one who has a personal witness, by one who has had experience with the Spirit of the Lord. We often begin our spiritual development by relying on and trusting in the witness of others. On more than one occasion, I heard Elder Harold B. Lee say to groups of missionaries: "Elders and sisters, if the time comes when you are shaken, when you wonder or doubt, when you don't know for sure, then lean on my witness, because I do know." I leaned on the testimony of my mother and father. When I was in the depths of despair and shaken to the core over anti-Mormon material, one of the things to which I held tenaciously was the witness of my parents. More specifically, I knew that my dad knew. He was a good man. I knew that. He wouldn't believe in something or commit himself to it if it were false. I knew that. And so I leaned on his faith until I acquired a witness of my own. In fact, the revelations affirm that "to some it is given by the Holy Ghost to know that Jesus Christ is the Son of God, and that he was crucified for the sins of the world. To others it is given to believe on their words, that they also might have eternal life if they continue faithful." (D&C 46:13–14.) Like Alma, those who pray and search and read and study and inquire—those who follow the course of gaining a witness—come in time to know, to know as surely as they know they live. It is the promise of God to all. He is no respecter of persons. He knows, and he wants all his children to know as he knows. Truly, as Moroni explained, it is "by the power of the Holy Ghost [that we] may *know* the truth of all things." (Moroni 10:5; italics added.)

Declaring the Witness

One struggle that my missionary companion and I had while we were wrestling with our testimonies was our inability, as we supposed, to bear testimony of something about which we were not certain. Is such proper? Is it not hypocritical? Elder Boyd K. Packer addressed this question. "It is not unusual," he observed, "to have a missionary say, 'How can I bear testimony until I get one? How can I testify that God lives, that Jesus is the Christ and that the gospel is true? If I do not have such a testimony would that not be dishonest?'

"Oh, if I could teach you this one principle! A testimony is to be *found* in the *bearing* of it. Somewhere in your quest for spiritual knowledge, there is that 'leap of faith,' as the philosophers call it. It is the moment when you have gone to the edge of the light and step into the darkness to discover that the way is lighted ahead for just a footstep or two. The spirit of man, as the scripture says, indeed is the candle of the Lord.

"It is one thing to receive a witness from what you have read or what another has said; and that is a necessary beginning. It is quite another to have the Spirit confirm to you in your bosom that what *you* have testified is true. Can you not see that it will be supplied as you share it? As you give that which you have, there is a replacement, with increase!" (*"That All May Be Edified,"* pp. 339–40; italics in original.)

I have been interested over the years in the manner in which testimonies are borne. Let me share an experience which, though painful, started me on a course that greatly aided my comprehension of what it means to bear witness of the truth. While serving in a stake presidency, I had responsibility for the youth programs of the stake. One year I worked closely with the stake Young Men's and Young Women's presidents in planning a youth conference. Because the young people of the stake were so spread out, because they saw one another so seldom, we wanted this two-day conference to be just right, to combine the elements of sociality and spirituality in such a way as to make a real difference in the lives of the youth. All the events of Saturday morning and evening, including a dance, went well. And now we wanted more than anything for the testimony meeting, held early Sunday morning, to be the highlight of the conference. Special musical numbers had been arranged. The setting had been prepared. I asked the Young Men's and Young Women's presidents to stand at the beginning of the meeting and bear brief, heartfelt testimonies, to set the tone of the meeting and to model what we hoped would follow.

There was a brief pause after the Young Women's president bore her testimony. Then the youth became involved. A young woman from one of the distant branches spoke: "I want to stand and bear my testimony. I want to tell Laura (a young woman to whom she pointed) how much I love her. I want her to know how much she means to me." The speaker was very emotional but managed to spend about ten minutes telling stories about herself and Laura. She closed. At that point Laura stood up, came to the pulpit, and said: "I want to bear my testimony. I want to tell Stephanie how much I love her." She cried and cried as she told stories about how the two of them had romped and played as little children and about how close they were. Before she sat down, she added, "Oh, I also need to tell Bill what a difference he has made in my life. He's been a wonderful friend to Stephanie and me. We love you, Bill." As we might guess, Stephanie was followed by Bill, who was followed by the person about whom Bill spoke, and so on for about forty-five minutes. This approach to things was broken suddenly by one young woman striding up to the stand and with much confidence saying: "I've been thinking about this meeting for some time, wondering what I should speak about, and so I went to my Mom and asked her what I should say. My mother suggested that I tell you what her Catholic priest taught her: 'Every time we sin, we drive the crown of thorns deeper into the skull of Jesus.'" She then encouraged us as a congregation to avoid sin. At this point the stake president, who sat two chairs from me, let out a quiet groan that indicated his disappointment with the meeting. But frankly, things had been going fine compared with where they headed for the next little while! A young man from one of the local wards came up to the pulpit carrying a folder. He opened the folder, took out several legal-sized sheets of paper, and began: "My talk today is on the sacrament." He then delivered an eleven-minute sermon on the importance of the Sacrament of the Lord's Supper, on the need for being worthy to take the bread and water each Sunday, and on the meaning of taking upon us the name of Christ. It was really quite a good talk.

At about the midpoint of the meeting, a young man came to the stand and took charge for about twenty-five minutes: he began by telling a few jokes, told a number of sad stories, and then, having elicited both laughter and tears, said: "Hey, I'm pretty good at this. I think I'll be an entertainer!" The congregation roared. At least most of them did. The stake president groaned again. He slipped me a note that said simply: "This meeting is a disaster." I nodded to him my agreement of his assessment. I perspired. The Young

Women's president wept. The Young Men's president sighed. I wasn't sure what to do, whether to close the meeting, cast out the strange spirit there, or simply get up and explain what was wrong. The stake leaders, all of us, knew that this was a sensitive time, that feelings were delicate, that persons are easily hurt or their efforts easily stifled. So we did nothing. We sat. And we sat. Painfully, we sat.

After about two hours, a young man whom we did not recognize walked to the pulpit. He was extremely nervous, so much so that he dared not even lift his head to look at the congregation. He stammered: "My friends, or, uh ... brothers and sisters, I ... uh ... would like to ... uh ... share some of my feelings. I am not a Mormon, not a member of your church, and so I don't really know how to bear testimony." The stake president, one of the most Christ-like men I have ever known, whispered: "He should relax. He's in great company!" The young man continued: "The missionaries have been teaching my family about your church for a couple of weeks now. I just wanted to let you know that I really believe in God. I feel a lot of love for Jesus, who died for me. Something inside me tells me that what the missionaries have said about Joseph Smith and the Book of Mormon and the Mormon Church is true. I'm happy that in a short time we will be baptized. Thank you for being so nice to me." Then he sat down. Here was a testimony, a real testimony, and it came from the only nonmember in the group.

The meeting did finally come to an end. Mercifully, after almost three hours, it came to an end. I sat in despair. So did the other stake leaders. The stake president looked at me, shook his head in disbelief, and sighed. Then he left. I turned to the stake youth leaders and said, "I'm too depressed to talk about it now. Could we meet this Wednesday evening in my office?" They agreed that we would face the music then. It was clear from the looks on their faces on Wednesday that they had spent a great deal of time in ponderous and solemn thought. So had I. Interestingly enough, each of us had had occasion on Sunday to return to our own wards and participate in the monthly fast and testimony meeting. And so I asked: "Is this a youth problem?" The Young Women's president quickly spoke up: "No, it's a Church problem." She continued: "The kids do basically the same things the adults do. Perhaps the grownups are a bit more dignified and formal about it." The Young Men's president nodded in agreement. I indicated that those were my feelings as well. We sat for a long time that night, asking such questions as, What's supposed to happen in a testimony meeting? What is appropriate, and what is inappropriate? Are there some expressions that are perfectly right and good in one setting but not quite right for a testimony meeting? Why was the spirit of the youth meeting so strange? Why did so many of the youth feel it was inspirational? Are we the ones who are out of it, insensitive to what we ought to feel? And so on. It was a sober occasion for the three of us, a vexation of the soul, painful searching after truth. We felt the need thereafter to express our concerns to the stake president and to suggest that a message be prepared and delivered by him (or whomever he recommended) on the matter of acquiring and bearing testimony, a message for the whole stake membership. As a stake presidency we first instructed the bishops and high council, turning to the scriptures and the words of living apostles and prophets for our pattern. We stressed the need for being delicate and sensitive, of never indicating that there was one "approved" way of bearing witness, a "proper" approach to sharing one's testimony. Rather, we strove to speak in terms of correct principles. I think some good came from the whole thing.

Seldom in my life have I spent as much time in serious reflection on a matter as I did in the weeks and months that followed that youth testimony meeting. Seldom in my life have I pondered and searched to understand the meaning and purpose of a meeting. I thought back on a thousand testimony meetings I had attended and of the unusual things that had taken place there. I thought of my Sunday School teacher when I was twelve, a lovely young woman who loved the Lord and lived his gospel. It showed. I distinctly remember that every month in fast and testimony meeting she would stand up and say: "I'd like to read a message from the *Improvement Era*." She would then read an article to the congregation. I thought it was what she was supposed to do—perhaps it was her church assignment or something. She did that month after month, year after year. I thought back to a middle-aged woman standing up in testimony meeting and, with fire in her eyes and voice, saying to all of us: "You hypocrites! You phonies! You claim to be Christians. That's a joke!" She went on to tear apart the ward for not being more helpful in fellowshipping her nonmember husband. I reflected on a man standing up in testimony meeting and startling us with, "As many of you know, I teach the fourteen-year-olds in Sunday School. I wasn't able to finish my lesson in time today, and so I'd like to do that now, if it's okay with the rest of you." He then took about fifteen minutes to complete his Sunday School lesson.

A few years ago in one of my Book of Mormon classes at Brigham Young University, after I had finished a discussion of Alma 4:19 and the matter of bearing pure testimony, a student spoke to me after class. He said: "Brother Millet, I wanted so badly to bear my testimony in yesterday's fast meeting in my BYU ward, but I didn't have anything original to say. I didn't have a special message to deliver." This experience highlights a problem we sometimes see in the Church: the presumption that one has to deliver a message, preach a sermon, or make some original contribution to the meeting. The *General Handbook of Instructions* simply indicates that members of the Church are to be invited to bear brief, heartfelt testimonies and, where appropriate, share faith-promoting experiences. There really is no need for the members of the Church to worry one-tenth of a second about coming up with something to say, about leaving the congregation with a lasting message, about giving a talk. I frequently ask groups of returned missionaries the following questions: "Did you ever have any inspirational testimony meetings on your mission?" They inevitably respond: "Oh yes. We had some great ones!" I continue: "I'll bet they were spiritual feasts because every elder or sister said something different. Right?" "Not usually," they answer. "I'll bet they were unusual spiritual experiences because each missionary came with a prepared sermon, delivered it effectively, and set the other missionaries back on their heels with the power of his or her oratory. Right?" "Not really," they respond. "Well, then, what did the missionaries say as part of their expressions?" After a few moments' reflection, the class relates that most of the elders and sisters said about the same thing— they bore testimony of God, of Jesus as the Christ, of Joseph Smith and the Book of Mormon, and of the guiding hand of the Lord in the Church today. Very little original stuff. But powerful. There's a lesson there.

As I understand it, the purpose of a testimony meeting is for the bearing of personal testimony. Expressions of gratitude and love, so much a part of the lives of followers of the Christ, take a backseat to the bearing of testimonies if in fact the meeting has been set aside for the bearing of testimonies. Letting others know how thankful we are for our blessings, as well as how much we love the Lord and one another—these expressions can and should accompany our testimony, but we are asked primarily to stand and bear witness of what we know to be true. President Spencer W. Kimball counseled a group of young people gathered in a testimony meeting: "Do not exhort each other; that is not a testimony. Do not tell others how to live. *Just tell how you feel inside. That is the testimony.* The moment you begin preaching to others, your testimony ended. *Just tell us how you feel,* what your mind and heart and every fiber of your body tells you." (*Teachings of Spencer W. Kimball,* p. 138; italics added.) On another occasion, President Kimball said to a similar group: "Now, you are going to give your testimonies this afternoon. I hope that you'll just open your hearts and let us look inside . . . will you? Just open them up wide and turn on the lights and let us see your hearts . . . how you feel. *A testimony is not an exhortation; a testimony is not a sermon; none of you are here to exhort the rest. You are here to bear your own witness.* It is amazing what you can say in thirty seconds by way of testimony, or in sixty seconds, or one hundred and twenty, or two hundred and forty, or whatever time you are given, if you confine yourselves to testimony. We'd like to know how you feel." (Unpublished address delivered in Los Angeles, California, 2 Jan. 1959, p. 9, as cited in *Testimony,* comp. H. Stephen Stoker and Joseph C. Muren, p. 139; italics added.)

I've thought many times of the emotion that was evident in the youth testimony meeting. I've been troubled over the years that too often our youth (and, unfortunately, some of our more experienced members) are prone to confuse sentimentality with spirituality, tears with testimony. Let me illustrate. One Mutual night as I came out of my bishop's office, I noticed that the Laurel class was huddled in the hall in the midst of what seemed to be quite a fascinating discussion. They appeared to be talking about one of the young women in their class who had during the last year slipped out of activity in the Church. I heard one of the young women say, with some enthusiasm, "Well, I can tell you this much—she doesn't have much of a testimony." One of the others challenged her. "How can you say that? How do you know?" The first replied, "Well, think about it for a minute. I've seen her bear her testimony many times, and I've never seen her cry once!" There was a pause, a moment of reflection on the part of twelve young women, and then a rather visible concurrence. Most of them nodded in agreement and said, "She's right about that." I was flabbergasted.

Almost twenty years ago I taught several classes of eleventh graders in seminary. My fourth-period class was a remarkable group. During the first part of the year, however, I noticed something a bit unusual. Day after day for about three weeks I noticed that every devotional to start the class and set the spiritual tone involved some kind of death story. Somebody was dying or giving their life or blood or something. I pulled the class president aside after the third week and asked: "Fred, what's the deal with the devotionals?" He didn't follow me. "I mean, why all the morbid stories in our devotionals? Why are we so hung up on death?" Fred responded verbally in a polite manner, but the look on his face betrayed the fact that my question had totally mystified him. "Brother Millet," he came right back, "How else are we going to get the kids to cry?" I said, "Oh, I understand." I didn't follow up on the conversation at the time; I felt it best to wait until I had thought through my response.

There's no question that when we have a genuine spiritual experience, we may be touched emotionally. Tears come easily for some of us, and there should never be the slightest embarrassment about such a thing. And yet we do ourselves and our youth a tremendous disservice if we begin to believe that an emotional experience is always a spiritual experience. Tears may come, but they should never be manipulated or elicited or sought for. In the classroom, for example, there is plenty for the gospel teacher to do by way of study, prayer, preparation, organization, and presentation; he or she must not seek to usurp the role of the Holy Ghost. He is the Comforter. He is the Revelator. He is the Converter. He is, in reality, the Teacher. We strive to be an instrument. We may seek and pray for an outpouring of the Spirit, but we must never attempt to manufacture the same. President Howard W. Hunter, in speaking to Church Educational System personnel, said:

"In one of the most basic revelations of this dispensation, the Lord said, 'And the Spirit shall be given unto you by the prayer of faith; and if ye receive not the Spirit ye shall not teach' (D&C 42:14).

"I take this verse to mean not only that we *should not* teach without the Spirit, but also that we really *cannot* teach without it. Learning of spiritual things simply cannot take place without the instructional and confirming presence of the Spirit of the Lord. . . .

"Let me offer a word of caution on this subject. I think if we are not careful as professional teachers working in the classroom every day, we may begin to try to counterfeit the true influence of the Spirit of the Lord by unworthy and manipulative means. I get concerned when it appears that strong emotion or free-flowing tears are equated with the presence of the Spirit. Certainly the Spirit of the Lord can bring strong emotional feelings, including tears, but that outward manifestation ought not be confused with the presence of the Spirit itself.

"I have watched a great many of my brethren over the years and we have shared some rare and unspeakable spiritual experiences together. Those experiences have all been different, each special in its own way, and such sacred moments may or may not be accompanied by tears. Very often they are, but sometimes they are accompanied by total silence. Other times they are accompanied by joy. Always they are accompanied by a great manifestation of the truth, of revelation to the heart.

"Give your students gospel truth powerfully taught; that is the way to give them a spiritual experience. Let it come naturally and as it will, perhaps with the shedding of tears, but perhaps not. If what you say is the truth, and you say it purely and with honest conviction, those students will feel the spirit of the truth being taught them and will recognize that inspiration and revelation has come into their hearts. That is how we build faith. That is how we strengthen testimonies — with the power of the word of God taught in purity and with conviction." ("Eternal Investments," address to CES personnel, 10 Feb. 1989, Salt Lake City, p. 3; italics in original.)

Though President Hunter's remarks were directed primarily to full-time religious educators, the principles he enunciates certainly apply to the bearing of pure testimony. Something remarkable takes place when the Latter-day

Saints bear pure testimony. A spiritual presence accompanies such expressions that can be felt in no other way, and there are outcomes that attest to the power and validity of doing so. Because of the growing waywardness of his people, Alma the Younger determined to leave the office of chief judge, or governor, and devote himself to the work of the ministry. Of this occasion, Mormon wrote: "And this he did that he himself might go forth among his people, or among the people of Nephi, that he might preach the word of God unto them, to stir them up in remembrance of their duty, and that he might pull down, by the word of God, all the pride and craftiness and all the contentions which were among his people, *seeing no way that he might reclaim them save it were in bearing down in pure testimony against them.*" (Alma 4:19; italics added.)

On the other hand, something is missing when the Latter-day Saints fail to bear pure testimony. Something is lost. Elder Boyd K. Packer spoke of a time when he presided over the New England Mission. "We held a series of zone conferences," he wrote, "to improve the spirituality in the mission. Rather than schedule instruction on the mechanics of missionary work, we determined to have a testimony meeting. In the last conference, in the testimony of one of the humble elders, I found the answer to the problem. There was something different about the brief testimony of this frightened new elder. He stood for less than a minute, yet I learned from his expression what it was that was missing.

"The testimonies we'd heard from all the other missionaries went something like this: 'I'm grateful to be in the mission field. I've learned a lot from it. I have a fine companion. I've learned a lot from him. I'm grateful for my parents. We had an interesting experience last week. We were out knocking on doors and . . . . ' Then the missionary would relate an experience. His conclusion would be something like this: 'I'm grateful to be in the mission field. I have a testimony of the gospel.' And he would conclude 'in the name of Jesus Christ. Amen.'

"This young elder was different somehow. Anxious not to spend an extra second on his feet, he said simply, in hurried, frightened words, 'I know that God lives. I know that Jesus is the Christ. I know that we have a prophet of God leading the Church. In the name of Jesus Christ. Amen.'

"This was a testimony. It was not just an experience nor an expression of gratitude. It was a declaration, a witness!

"Most of the elders had said 'I have a testimony,' but they had not declared it. This young elder had, in a very few words, delivered his testimony — direct, basic, and, as it turned out, powerful.

"I then knew what was wrong in the mission. We were telling stories, expressing gratitude, admitting that we had testimonies, but we were not bearing them." (*Teach Ye Diligently*, p. 275.)

A Witness Properly Rooted

I was asked some years ago by a mission president to speak to his missionaries at a zone conference. We had a lovely gathering and a fine exchange of ideas. I was invited to stay for lunch and visit with the missionaries. I did a great deal of listening and learned much. One of the most interesting conversations revolved around a young couple who were being taught by the missionaries but who were not progressing. "They're golden people," one elder said, "ripe and ready for membership in the Church. They just won't commit to be baptized."

Several suggestions were made by the missionaries listening in—fasting with them, having the bishop meet with them, intensifying the friendshipping effort, etc., to all of which the first elder said, "We've tried that."

After a long pause, one elder spoke up. "Have you given them the 'scrolls discussion'?"

The first elder responded, "No. Do you think this would be a good time for the 'scrolls discussion'?"

"Sounds like a perfect time to me," the first came back.

Now I had never heard of the "scrolls discussion." I was dying to know what it was, so I blurted out, "What's the 'scrolls discussion'?"

The second elder looked quizzically at me and said, "Surely, Brother Millet, you've heard of the 'scrolls discussion'?"

I indicated that I had not.

"The 'scrolls discussion,' " he said, "involves showing the people how the Dead Sea Scrolls prove the truthfulness of the Church!"

I asked, "How do you do that?"

"Well," he replied, "as you know, the Dead Sea Scrolls contain information about a group of Christians out in the deserts of Judea."

I said, "No, they don't. The Dead Sea Scrolls were written by a group of hyperreligious Jews."

He said, "Oh. I didn't know that." Then he followed up, "Well, you do know that they had three presiding high priests at the head of their church."

I indicated that the leaders of their group were Aaronic priests, not Melchizedek.

He went on. "Well, there's much doctrine within the scrolls that proves ours to be true."

I commented that the scrolls were interesting historical documents but did very little for us doctrinally.

This exchange went on for about ten minutes, the elder providing what he thought to be airtight "proofs" and I trying gently to let him know that most of what he understood about the Dead Sea Scrolls was simply untrue. I could see the frustration in his eyes. He breathed a sigh and then concluded the debate with, "Well, I'll just say this—the 'scrolls discussion' has always worked perfectly for me!"

I thought then (and have since) about all the people who may have come into the Church as a result of what they learned in the famous "scrolls discussion." I shuddered.

This is the Lord's church. It is built upon divine precepts and principles, founded on diamond truth and God-given authority. It needs no props. We need not stretch nor sensationalize nor intellectualize the message of the Restoration to make it more palatable. It will stand on its own. Joseph Smith taught that truth cuts its own way. (*Teachings of the Prophet Joseph Smith,* p. 313.) Our witness of the truth—a sign of our spiritual maturity in the faith—must be grounded in substance, in true doctrine, in that which will endure the test of time. My friend who almost left the Church because of archaeological evidences of the Book of Mormon had not paid a sufficient price to know by the power of the Holy Ghost that the Book of Mormon is the word of God; consequently, he was found wanting at the moment of trial. We may have a testimony of many things—of the programs and procedures and policies of the Restored Church—and yet not be settled in truth. There are some things which we must come to know, know with an assurance borne of the Spirit, if we are to endure the tests that will come. We need to know that there is a God in heaven, that he is infinite and eternal, and that he is our Parent, the Father of the spirits of all men and women. We need to know that Jesus is the Christ, that he is literally the Only Begotten Son of the Father in the flesh, and that salvation comes by him and through him and in no other way. We need to know that Joseph Smith was and is a prophet of God, that he is a revealer of truth and a legal administrator, that knowledge and authority have been delivered to earth in this final gospel dispensation through his instrumentality. We need to know that the revelations and translations given through Joseph the Seer, especially the Book of Mormon, are true and from God, that they contain the mind and will and voice of the Almighty to those who live in this last age of the earth's history. Finally, we need to know that The Church of Jesus Christ of Latter-day Saints is, in the language of the revelation, the only true and living Church on the face of the earth (D&C 1:30), is the kingdom of God on earth, is in the line of its duty, and is preparing a people for the second coming of the Son of Man. These things matter. They matter a great deal. Our testimonies will be intact and solid to the degree that they are grounded in these essential verities.

Though we may begin simply in the development of our witness, though at first what we testify to be true may be based more upon feeling than upon knowledge, the Lord expects his servants to search and study and grow in understanding, to acquire a reason for the hope that is within them. (See 1 Peter 3:15.) Simply stated, the Spirit bears witness of truth, of substantive realities. "The sanctity of a true testimony," President Joseph F. Smith counseled the Church, "should inspire a thoughtful care as to its use. That testimony is not to be forced upon everybody, nor is it to be proclaimed at large from the housetop. It is not to be voiced merely to 'fill up the time' in a public meeting; far less to excuse or disguise the speaker's poverty of thought or ignorance of the truth he is called to expound. . . . Of those who speak in his name, the Lord requires humility, not ignorance." (*Gospel Doctrine*, pp. 205–6.)

In this day we have been commanded to be true and loyal to the Restoration, to bear testimony of those things that have come by and through Joseph Smith. (See D&C 31:4; 49:1–4.) Indeed, the Lord has warned us as a people of the condemnation, scourge, and judgment—surely the lost spiritual privileges and opportunities—that rest upon the Church because of our near neglect of the Book of Mormon and modern revelations. The Savior has also instructed us how we may extricate ourselves from this spiritual plight: "I will forgive you of your sins with this commandment—that you remain steadfast in your minds in solemnity and the spirit of prayer, in bearing testimony to all the world of those things which are communicated unto you." (D&C 84:61.) Occasionally we hear people complain that they hear too few testimonies of Christ and too many of Joseph Smith. To be sure, we worship the Father in the name of the Son; Christ our Lord is the way to the Father, and his is the only name under heaven whereby we can be saved. And yet the head of the dispensation is the preeminent revealer of Christ to the world in his day. Thus to bear witness of Joseph Smith is to bear witness of Jesus Christ, who sent him, in the same way that a testimony of Christ also implies clearly a testimony of the Eternal Father, who sent Christ. I have observed that there is a power—an unusual spiritual endowment from that Lord we worship—associated with the bearing of a pure and fervent testimony of Joseph Smith and the Restoration. Such outpourings surely signify heaven's approbation.

President David O. McKay's father learned, as a young missionary, of the importance of bearing testimony of the choice seer. After laboring in a town in Scotland he had decided, because of persecution, to speak of Christ and Christian principles and to postpone for the time being his discussion of the Restoration. He thereafter experienced a gloom and darkness of soul that he had never known, a pall of bitterness so intense that he concluded either he would have it removed or he would leave his labors and return home. In pleading and sober prayer he called upon God for deliverance. The Spirit spoke: "Testify that Joseph Smith is a prophet of God." The darkness was lifted, and Elder McKay continued his ministry. (See *Gospel Ideals,* pp. 21–22.) In this same spirit, Elder Matthew Cowley, before leaving on his first mission, was given the following counsel from his father: "My boy, you will go out on that mission; you will study; you will try to prepare your sermons; and sometimes when you are called upon, you will think you are wonderfully prepared, but when you stand up, your mind will go completely blank."

Young Elder Cowley asked what he should do in such circumstances. His father said, " 'You stand up there and with all the fervor of your soul, you bear witness that Joseph Smith was a prophet of the living God, and thoughts will flood into your mind and words to your mouth, to round out those thoughts in a facility of expression that will carry conviction to the heart of everyone who listens.' And so my mind, being mostly blank during my five years in the mission field, gave me the opportunity to bear testimony to the greatest event in the history of the world since the crucifixion of the Master." (*Matthew Cowley Speaks,* p. 298.)

There is no way, given our limited perspective in this life, that we can measure the eternal influence of pure testimony.

Perhaps only when we are able to look back on the whole of our existence, able to see things as they really are, from God Almighty's point of view, will we be able to sense and feel the powerful coalescence of circumstances, the divinely contrived orchestration of people and events. Perhaps then we will be in a position to measure just how much difference has been made by human testimony. Some testimonies shake the earth.

I remember very well the feeling of deep, personal loss when I learned of the passing of President David O. McKay in January 1970. He had been the prophet of my youth, the only president of the Church I really remembered. I worried about my ability to shift allegiance and commitment to President Joseph Fielding Smith, his successor. I prayed and prayed to have the same witness about President Smith's call that I had felt about President McKay's. By the time the April 1970 general conference convened, I still had not received what was to me a sufficient confirmation that the will of the Lord had been done. Things changed dramatically for me, however, when I heard President Smith speak the following words at the close of the conference:

"I desire to say that no man of himself can lead this church. It is the Church of the Lord Jesus Christ; he is at the head. The Church bears his name, has his priesthood, administers his gospel, preaches his doctrine, and does his work.

"He chooses men and calls them to be instruments in his hands to accomplish his purposes, and he guides and directs them in their labors. But men are only instruments in the Lord's hands, and the honor and glory for all that his servants accomplish is and should be ascribed unto him forever. If this were the work of man, it would fail, but it is the work of the

Lord, and he does not fail." (In Conference Report, Apr. 1970, p. 113.)

Something happened to me as a result of hearing that sweet but direct testimony, something that has affected my life permanently. I saw the power of God resting upon President Joseph Fielding Smith; that witness went down into my heart and burned like fire. It has happened in like manner on subsequent occasions as new prophets have been chosen and appointed. I remember also a time some two and a half years later, at the October 1972 general conference, when President Harold B. Lee was sustained as the eleventh president of the Church and a new apostle, Elder Bruce R. McConkie, was called. This new special witness declared: "As members of the church and kingdom of God on earth, we enjoy the gifts of the Spirit — those wonders and glories and miracles that a gracious and benevolent God always has bestowed upon his faithful saints. The first of these gifts listed in our modern revelation on spiritual gifts is the gift of testimony, the gift of revelation, the gift of knowing of the truth and divinity of the work. This gift is elsewhere described as the testimony of Jesus, which is the spirit of prophecy. This is my gift. I know this work is true.

"I have a perfect knowledge that Jesus Christ is the Son of the living God and that he was crucified for the sins of the world. I know that Joseph Smith is a prophet of God through whose instrumentality the fullness of the everlasting gospel has been restored again in our day. And I know that this Church of Jesus Christ of Latter-day Saints is the kingdom of God on earth." (In Conference Report, Oct. 1972, p. 21.)

I was moved and strengthened by that witness in ways that I cannot explain. I knew, with a knowledge more powerful than sight, that he knew.

More than twelve years later that same apostle delivered to the Church his last testimony, one that has touched and will yet touch the hearts of millions of people across the globe. "And now," he affirmed, in speaking of the redemption of Christ, "as pertaining to this perfect atonement, wrought by the shedding of the blood of God—I testify that it took place in Gethsemane and at Golgotha, and as pertaining to Jesus Christ, I testify that he is the Son of the Living God and was crucified for the sins of the world. He is our Lord, our God, and our King. This I know of myself independent of any other person.

"I am one of his witnesses, and in a coming day I shall feel the nail marks in his hands and in his feet and shall wet his feet with my tears.

"But I shall not know any better then than I know now that he is God's Almighty Son, that he is our Savior and Redeemer, and that salvation comes in and through his atoning blood and in no other way." (In Conference Report, Apr. 1985, p. 12.)

Who among us who heard this final earthly apostolic witness of Elder Bruce R. McConkie will ever be the same? Indeed, the witness of the Brethren not only provides sustenance and support for our own developing testimonies but also stands as a pattern and a guide to how the Lord expects his Saints to bear pure testimony.

As we develop line upon line, as we grow here a little and there a little in our witness of the work in which we are engaged, we are becoming steadfast and immovable. Like Jacob, son of Lehi, because of our experience with the Spirit of the Lord, we will be unshaken in the faith when we encounter antichrists and the doctrine of devils. (Jacob 7:5.)

And, like Enos, Jacob's son, because we will have heard the word of the Lord and have come to treasure above all else those matters of eternal import, our faith will begin to be unshaken in the Lord. (Enos 1:11.) We will have begun to mature in our convictions.

Chapter Four

Growing in the Pure Love of Christ

One sign of spiritual maturity is an expansion of our capacity to love—to love God and our fellowmen. People are the Lord's most important product, and as long as we are involved in the work of the Lord, we will and should be involved in the work of blessing people. Those who come out of the world into the true Church—who forsake their sins, who take upon them the name of Christ—covenant to live a life consistent with the doctrines and principles espoused and exemplified by the Master. They covenant to be Christians. They covenant to love.

To those who have gotten onto the strait and narrow path that leads to eternal life, Nephi counsels: "Wherefore, ye must press forward with a steadfastness in Christ, having a perfect brightness of hope, and *a love of God and of all men.* Wherefore, if ye shall press forward, feasting upon the word of Christ, and endure to the end, behold, thus saith the Father: Ye shall have eternal life." (2 Nephi 31:20; italics added.) In this single phrase, "love of God," we see both divine and human initiative.

God's Love for Us

Godlike love begins with and centers in and emanates from God. The apostle John wrote that "God is love; and he that dwelleth in love dwelleth in God, and God in him." (1 John 4:16.) Our Heavenly Father and his Only Begotten Son, Jesus Christ, possess in perfection all of the attributes of godliness, including charity. They love purely, absolutely, and perfectly. Moroni, speaking to the Savior, said: "And again, I remember that thou hast said that thou hast loved the world, even unto the laying down of thy life for the world, that thou mightest take it again to prepare a place for the children of men. And now I know that *this love which thou hast had for the children of men is charity.*" (Ether 12:33–34; italics added.) Pure love comes from a pure source, from God. It begins with God, is extended by him to man, and sheds "itself abroad in the hearts of the children of men." (1 Nephi 11:22.) As we shall see, we are able to love others purely only as we seek for and partake of the love of God ourselves. As the Prophet Joseph Smith explained, "Love is one of the chief characteristics of Deity, and ought to be manifested by those who aspire to be the sons of God." (*Teachings of the Prophet Joseph Smith,* p. 174.)

One of the greatest evidences of the Father's love for us is in the gift of his Beloved Son. The prophet Nephi, having desired to receive the same manifestation that his father Lehi had been given, was shown a vision of a rod of iron, a strait and narrow path, and a large and spacious building. In addition, he beheld a tree whose beauty was "far beyond, yea, exceeding of all beauty; and the whiteness thereof did exceed the whiteness of the driven snow." (1 Nephi 11:8.) Lehi had explained that the fruit "was most sweet, above all that [he] ever before tasted." Further, "it filled [his] soul with exceedingly great joy." (1 Nephi 8:11–12.) Nephi concluded from his visionary experience that the tree represented "the love of God, which sheddeth itself abroad in the hearts of the children of men; wherefore, it is the most desirable above all things." Nephi's guide, an angel, added, "Yea, and the most joyous to the soul." (1 Nephi 11:22–23.)

Earlier in this same chapter, it is written that the Spirit asked Nephi, "Believest thou that thy father saw the tree of which he hath spoken?" Nephi answered, "Yea, thou knowest that I believe all the words of my father." And then the Spirit exulted: "Hosanna to the Lord, the most high God; for he is God over all the earth, yea, even above all. And *blessed art thou, Nephi, because thou believest in the Son of the most high God.* ... And behold," the Spirit continued, "this thing shall be given unto thee for *a sign,* that after thou hast beheld *the tree* which bore the fruit which thy father tasted, thou shalt also behold *a man* descending out of heaven, and him shall ye witness; and after ye have witnessed him *ye shall bear record that it is the Son of God.*" (1 Nephi 11:4–7; italics added.) This tree was more than an abstract principle, more than a vague sentiment, albeit a divine sentiment. The tree was a doctrinal symbol, a "sign" of an even greater reality—a type of him whose branches provide shade from the scorching rays of sin and ignorance. This was a messianic message, a poignant prophecy of him toward whom all men and women press on that path which leads eventually to life eternal. Truly God the Father "so loved the world, that he gave his only begotten Son, that whosoever believeth in him should not perish, but have everlasting life." (John 3:16; compare 1 John 4:9; D&C 34:3.)

Our Love for God

John the Beloved observed that we love God because he
first loved us. (See 1 John 4:10, 19.) "To love God with all
your heart, soul, mind, and strength," President Ezra Taft
Benson has taught, "is all-consuming and all-encompass-
ing. . . . The breadth, depth, and height of this love of God
extend into every facet of one's life. Our desires, be they
spiritual or temporal, should be rooted in a love of the Lord."
(*Teachings of Ezra Taft Benson,* p. 349.) As we live in a manner
that allows the Spirit to be with us regularly, we begin to see
things as they really are. Our love for God grows as we begin
to sense his goodness to us, as we become aware of his involvement in our lives, as we begin to acknowledge his hand
in all that is noble and good and worthy.

There are times when our love for God is almost consuming. Such feelings may come in prayer as we sense a
closeness through the Spirit to the Almighty. Sometimes such
feelings of gratitude come as we sing "Because I have Been
Given Much" (*Hymns,* no. 219) or "I Stand All Amazed"
(*Hymns,* no. 193) or "How Great Thou Art" (*Hymns,* no. 86),
or any number of other hymns that also allow our souls to
express praise or thanksgiving. Sometimes a love of the Lord
burns within us as we hear and feel the power of the word
as it is preached by one who does so under the direction of
the Holy Ghost. As we feel charity in the form of a pure love
for the Lord, we may, like Alma, feel to "sing the song of
redeeming love." (Alma 5:26.) To sing the song of redeeming
love is to joy in the matchless majesty of God's goodness, to
know the wonder of his love. It is to sense and know that the
Lord is intimately involved with his children and that he cares,
really cares, about their well-being. Jacob surely sang the song
of redeeming love when he exulted in the wisdom of God,

the greatness and justice of God, the mercy of God, the goodness of God, and the holiness of God. (See 2 Nephi 9.) Elder George F. Richards sought to explain the ineffable sense of love and gratitude that one can feel for his Lord and Savior: "More than forty years ago I had a dream which I am sure was from the Lord. In this dream I was in the presence of my Savior as he stood in mid-air. He spoke no word to me, but *my love for him was such that I have not words to explain. I know that no mortal man can love the Lord as I experienced that love for the Savior unless God reveals it to him.* I would have remained in his presence, but there was a power drawing me away from him.

"As a result of that dream, I had this feeling that no matter what might be required of my hands, what the gospel might entail unto me, I would do what I should be asked to do even to the laying down of my life. . . . If only I can be with my Savior and have that same sense of love that I had in that dream, it will be the goal of my existence, the desire of my life." (As cited by Spencer W. Kimball, in Conference Report, Apr. 1974, pp. 173–74; italics added.)

In that same spirit, Joseph Smith explained that following his first vision: "My Soul was filled with love and for many days I could rejoice with great joy and the Lord was with me." (From 1832 account, in Milton V. Backman, Jr., *Joseph Smith's First Vision,* p. 157.)

It is not only those who have seen the Lord — have enjoyed a personal appearance, a dream, or a vision — who feel the desire to sing the song of redeeming love. All those who have had the burdens of sin, the weight of guilt, and the agonies of bitterness, hostility, or pain removed by the Great Physician shout praises to the Holy One of Israel. They know that pure love of Christ. Nephi wrote: "My God hath been my support; he hath led me through mine afflictions in the wilderness; and he hath preserved me upon the waters of the great deep. He hath filled me with his love, even unto the consuming of my flesh." (2 Nephi 4:20–21.) And perhaps nowhere in holy writ do we find a more glorious expression of love and gratitude and praise of the Almighty than in the words of Ammon, son of Mosiah. "Blessed be the name of our God," he exulted to his brothers after the miraculous conversion of thousands of Lamanites. "Let us sing to his praise, yea, let us give thanks to his holy name, for he doth work righteousness forever. . . . Yea, we have reason to praise him forever, for he is the Most High God, and has loosed our brethren from the chains of hell. . . . Behold, who can glory too much in the Lord? Yea, who can say too much of his great power, and of his mercy, and of his long-suffering towards the children of men? Behold, I say unto you, I cannot say the smallest part which I feel." (Alma 26:8, 14, 16.)

Our Love for Others

One dramatic evidence of apostasy in the world today is a growing indifference toward and among the sons and daughters of God. "Because iniquity shall abound," the Savior taught before his death, "the love of men shall wax cold." (Joseph Smith–Matthew 1:30; compare D&C 45:27.) "It is one evidence," the Prophet Joseph Smith explained, "that men are unacquainted with the principles of godliness to behold the contraction [shrinking] of affectionate feelings and lack of charity in the world." On the other hand, those who come unto Christ become as Christ. They partake of his divine nature, receive his attributes, and come to love as he loves. "The nearer we get to our heavenly Father," the modern seer went on to say, "the more we are disposed to look with compassion on perishing souls; we feel that we want to take them upon our shoulders, and cast their sins behind our backs." (*Teachings of the Prophet Joseph Smith,* pp. 240–41.)

Ethical deeds, works of faith, acts of kindness toward others—these are so much more effective and pure when grounded in the love of Deity, that is, when the source of the goodness is the Holy One. As we begin to become new creatures in Christ, then we begin to serve out of proper motives. Nephi wrote that the Lord does not do anything "save it be for the benefit of the world; for he loveth the world, even that he layeth down his own life that he may draw all men unto him." Nephi then asks: "Hath he commanded any that they should not partake of his salvation? Behold I say unto you, Nay; but he hath given it free for all men." Nephi then explains that it must be on the basis of this same motivation— this charity, or pure love of Christ—that the people of the Lord labor in order for Zion to be established. Those who practice priestcraft, he observed, "preach and set themselves up for a light unto the world, that they may get gain and praise of the world; but they seek not the welfare of Zion." In this context we learn of charity as the antidote to priest-craft, the preventive medicine and the solution to improper or perverted desires: "The Lord God hath given a com-mandment that all men should have charity, which charity is love. And except they should have charity they were nothing. Wherefore, if they should have charity they would not suffer the laborer in Zion to perish. But the laborer in Zion shall labor for Zion; for if they labor for money they shall perish." (2 Nephi 26:24–31.)

Both Mormon (Moroni 7:45–48) and Paul (1 Corinthians 13:1–13) wrote of charity as the greatest of all the spiritual gifts, the one which shall endure forever. Both of them described the charitable person as one who:

1. *Suffers long; bears all things.* Charitable persons are endowed with a portion of the love of God and thus, to some degree, with the patience and perspective of God toward people and circumstances. Their vision of here and now (the present) is greatly affected by their glimpse of there and then (the future). It was by means of this pure love of Christ, which followed their spiritual rebirth (Mosiah 28:3), that Alma and the sons of Mosiah were able to bear the burdens that were placed upon them, even the burdens of persecution and rejection.

2. *Is kind.* Charity motivates to goodness, to benevolence and sensitivity toward the needs of others. People are the focus. It was by means of this pure love of Christ that Ammon, son of Mosiah, was able to extend himself, kindly and lovingly, in the service of Lamoni and his household, to win their hearts, and to be an instrument in their conversion to the truths of the gospel. (See Alma 17–19.)

3. *Envies not.* Those who love the Lord and are filled with his love are much less prone to concern themselves with the acquisitions or accolades of others. Their joy is full in Christ. (D&C 101:36.) They find happiness in simple pleasures and delight in God's goodness to them. It is by means of this pure love of Christ, this anchor to the soul, that people are able to ignore — to give no heed to — the tauntings and temptations of those who chant and proselyte from the great and spacious building. (See 1 Nephi 8.)

4. *Is not puffed up; seeks not one's own.* Charitable people seek diligently to turn attention away from themselves and toward God. They eagerly acknowledge the hand of the Lord in all things and hesitate to take personal credit for

accomplishments. Such individuals are devoid of pride. Mormon spoke of a time when many of the Nephites were lifted up in pride, so much so that they proved a major stumbling block to the Church, and the Church began to fail in its progress. At the same time, in that day of inequality and wickedness, there were others who, filled with the love of God, were "abasing themselves, succoring those who stood in need of their succor, such as imparting their substance to the poor and the needy, feeding the hungry, and suffering all manner of afflictions, for Christ's sake, who should come according to the spirit of prophecy." (Alma 4:13.)

5. *Is not easily provoked.* Those filled with the love of Christ are meek; theirs is a quiet but pervasive poise under provocation. Charity and an eternal perspective governed the reaction of Alma and Amulek when they were compelled to watch the hideous scene of women and children being burned to death. Their trust in Christ, and their confidence in the ultimate destiny of those who love and serve him, permitted them to witness even this horrible event with equanimity. Moreover, when an evil man later taunted them for their seeming inability to prevent the martyrdoms and "smote them with his hand upon their cheeks," they bore the abuse without complaint or angry response. As their Master would do more than a century later on another hemisphere, they stood with meek majesty before the assaults of the unholy. (See Alma 14.)

6. *Thinks no evil.* The minds of charitable individuals are on things of righteousness, their desire is for that which builds and strengthens and encourages. They have no secret agenda, no private yearnings for personal aggrandizement, only a heart focused on the Lord and his kingdom. "Behold," Nephi declared, "my soul delighteth in the things of the Lord; and

my heart pondereth continually upon the things which I have seen and heard." (2 Nephi 4:16.)

7. *Rejoices not in iniquity but rejoices in the truth.* Charitable persons are repulsed by sin, though anxious to fellowship and lift the sinner. They are pained by the waywardness of the world and labor tirelessly to extend gospel assistance to those who stray from the path of peace. At the same time, they delight in the Spirit, in goodness, in noble accomplishments and discoveries, no matter the source. Filled with a portion of the Lord's love, they, like the people of Benjamin, have no more disposition to do evil but rather to do good continually. (See Mosiah 5:2.) Though possessed with love for the wayward, they cannot look upon sin, save it be with abhorrence. (See Alma 13:12.)

8. *Believes all things.* It is not that those possessed of charity are naive or gullible; they are simply open to truth. They enjoy the spiritual gift of a believing heart and have little or no difficulty in accepting the words and following the counsel of those called to direct the destiny of the Church. Because they are believing in nature, all things work together for their good. (See D&C 90:24.) Like Sam, son of Lehi, charitable individuals readily believe on the testimony of one who knows. (See 1 Nephi 2:17; compare D&C 46:13–14.)

9. *Hopes all things.* Theirs is a hope in Christ, a quiet but dynamic assurance that even though they are imperfect, they are on course, that the Lord is pleased with their lives, that eternal life is at the end of the path. "What is it that ye shall hope for?" Mormon asked the humble followers of Christ. "Behold I say unto you that ye shall have hope through the atonement of Christ and the power of his resurrection, to be raised unto life eternal." (Moroni 7:41.)

10. *Endures all things.* No matter what the true followers

of Christ are required to pass through, they proceed as called. Neither the shame of the world nor the threat of physical death can deter those who are bent upon enjoying the love of God everlastingly. "If ye shall press forward," Nephi wrote, "feasting upon the word of Christ, and endure to the end, behold, thus saith the Father: Ye shall have eternal life." (2 Nephi 31:20.)

The greatest acts of charity come through the giving of oneself. Though there are times when money or food or material goods will meet a pressing need, the enduring need for sacrifice of self remains. "Never did the Savior give in expectation," President Spencer W. Kimball explained. "I know of no case in his life in which there was an exchange. He was always the giver, seldom the recipient. Never did he give shoes, hose, or a vehicle; never did he give perfume, a shirt, or a fur wrap. His gifts were of such a nature that the recipient could hardly exchange or return the value. His gifts were rare ones: eyes to the blind, ears to the deaf, and legs to the lame; cleanliness to the unclean, wholeness to the infirm, and breath to the lifeless. His gifts were opportunity to the downtrodden, freedom to the oppressed, light in the darkness, forgiveness to the repentant, hope to the despairing. His friends gave him shelter, food, and love. He gave them of himself, his love, his service, his life. The wise men brought him gold and frankincense. He gave them and all their fellow mortals resurrection, salvation, and eternal life. We should strive to give as he gave. To give of oneself is a holy gift." (*Teachings of Spencer W. Kimball,* pp. 246–47.)

It should go without saying that disciples of Christ ought to love one another. They have in common those things that matter most in life. Their view of reality, their goals and ambitions, their hopes and dreams for here and hereafter —

all these things they share with members of the Church far
and wide. They are welded together, clothed in the bond of
charity, that mantle "which is the bond of perfectness and
peace." (D&C 88:125.) The expression of the love of God is
not to be limited, however, to the household of faith. (See
D&C 121:45.) We have a duty beyond the fold as well, and
the Holy Spirit, which is the source of pure love, expands our
vision to see and feel as we ought. Joseph Smith said, "A
man filled with the love of God, is not content with blessing
his family alone, but ranges through the whole world, anxious
to bless the whole human race." (*Teachings of the Prophet
Joseph Smith,* p. 174.) On another occasion the Prophet declared: "There is a love from God that should be exercised
toward those of our faith, who walk uprightly, which is peculiar to itself, but it is without prejudice; *it also gives scope
to the mind, which enables us to conduct ourselves with greater
liberality towards all that are not of our faith,* than what they
exercise towards one another. These principles approximate
nearer to the mind of God, because it is like God, or God-
like." (*Teachings of the Prophet Joseph Smith,* p. 147; italics
added.) President Ezra Taft Benson thus observed that "we
must develop a love for people. Our hearts must go out to
them in the pure love of the gospel, in a desire to lift them,
to build them up, to point them to a higher, finer life and
eventually to exaltation in the celestial kingdom of God."
(*Come unto Christ,* p. 96.)

The Book of Mormon provides a companion witness of
the eternal fact that love of man is vitally related to love of
God, that when we are in the service of our fellow beings we
are only in the service of our God. (See Mosiah 2:17.) President Harold B. Lee related a personal experience that
brought this truth home to him in a powerful manner: "Just

before the dedication of the Los Angeles Temple," he said, "something new happened in my life when, along about three or four o'clock in the morning, I enjoyed an experience that I think was not a dream, but it must have been a vision. It seemed that I was witnessing a great spiritual gathering, where men and women were standing up, two or three at a time, and speaking in tongues. The spirit was so unusual. I seemed to hear the voice of President David O. McKay say, 'If you want to love God, you have to learn to love and serve the people. That is the way to show your love for God.' " (*Stand Ye in Holy Places,* p. 189.)

Indeed, the writers of holy writ affirm that service is essential to salvation. Benjamin taught that caring for the temporal and spiritual needs of the poor, for example, was inextricably tied to receiving the full blessings of the atonement of Christ. Having witnessed the marvelous manner in which the Spirit of the Lord pricked the hearts of those who hearkened to the words of his sermon; having listened as they called upon the name of the Lord for forgiveness of sin; having observed the people as their souls were transformed from guilt and remorse to joy and peace and love, Benjamin then explained how the Saints are enabled through service to remain clean before God. "*And now, for the sake of . . . retaining a remission of your sins from day to day,* that ye may walk guiltless before God—I would that *ye should impart of your substance to the poor,* every man according to that which he hath, such as feeding the hungry, clothing the naked, visiting the sick and administering to their relief, both spiritually and temporally, according to their wants." (Mosiah 4:26; italics added.) Mormon likewise spoke of a time in the days of Alma when the Saints were "abasing themselves, succoring those who stood in need of their succor, such as imparting their substance to the poor and the needy, . . . thus retaining a remission of their sins." (Alma 4:13–14.)

Obstacles to Charity

Because charity is so vital to the perfection of human nature and the growth of the kingdom of God, Satan labors incessantly to establish barriers or obstacles to the receipt and practice of this highest of spiritual gifts. Things get in the way to dam the flow of love from God to man, from man to God, and from man to man. Some of these include the following:

1. *Preoccupation with self.* Those who are preoccupied with self are unable to either feel the pure love of Christ or to extend that love to others. "The final and crowning virtue of the divine character," President Ezra Taft Benson explained, "is charity, or the pure love of Christ. (See Moroni 7:47.) If we would truly seek to be more like our Savior and Master, learning to love as He loves should be our highest goal. . . . The world today speaks a great deal about love, and it is sought for by many. But the pure love of Christ differs greatly from what the world thinks of love. Charity never seeks selfish gratification. The pure love of Christ seeks only the eternal growth and joy of others." (*Teachings of Ezra Taft Benson,* p. 275.) The Savior's commission to "love thy neighbour as thyself" (Matthew 19:19) has little to do with loving oneself; it has much to do with loving others as one would desire to be loved, to fulfill the Golden Rule as given by the Master in the sermon at Galilee and at Bountiful. (See Matthew 7:12; 3 Nephi 14:12.) There is no divine directive to spend time developing self-love or becoming obsessed with self-esteem. Rather, the irony of the ages is found in the

principle that only as one loses one's life does one find it. (See Matthew 16:25.)

2. *Dishonesty.* Only as we open ourselves to the truth, strive to know the truth, and then live in harmony with that truth can we grow in that love which is from God. In Dostoyevsky's classic work *The Brothers Karamazov,* Zossima says to Feodor: "A man who lies to himself and who listens to his own lies gets to a point where he can't distinguish any truth in himself or in those around him, and so loses all respect for himself and for others. Having no respect for anyone, he ceases to love, and to occupy and distract himself without love he becomes a prey to his passions and gives himself up to coarse pleasures, . . . and all this from continual lying to people and to himself. A man who lies to himself can be more easily offended than anyone else. For it is sometimes very pleasant to take offence, isn't it? And yet he knows that no one has offended him and that he has invented the offence himself, that he has lied just for the beauty of it, that he has exaggerated to make himself look big and important, that he has fastened on a phrase and made a mountain out of a molehill—he knows it all and yet is the first to take offence, he finds pleasure in it and feels mightily satisfied with himself, and so reaches the point of real enmity." (*The Brothers Karamazov,* p. 47.)

On the other hand, those persons, like Helaman's two thousand stripling warriors who are true at all times to themselves, to their values, to their witness, and to others (see Alma 53:20), come to know that true love which emanates from God and feel the need to be true to him. Of the Ammonites the Nephite record states, they were "distinguished for their zeal towards God, and also towards men; for *they were perfectly honest and upright in all things.*" Now note what follows: "And they were firm in the faith of Christ, even unto the end." (Alma 27:27; italics added.)

3. *Immorality.* Wickedness weakens love. Surely if god-like love is a spiritual gift, if it is bestowed as a result of faithfulness, then continuing in sin prevents one from receiving and giving such love. Sexual immorality, for example, prostitutes those God-given powers that are so intimately connected with the fountains of human life. Thus sexual expression outside the bonds of marriage estranges rather than builds and strengthens. Lust is a pitiful substitute for that love which is pure, that expression and that commitment which bind and seal throughout time and eternity. Jacob chastened his people, particularly the fathers and husbands, for their infidelity. "Ye have broken the hearts of your tender wives, and lost the confidence of your children," he said, "because of your bad examples before them; and the sobbings of their hearts ascend up to God against you." (Jacob 2:35.) The people of God are thus commanded to bridle all their passions, that they may be filled with love. (Alma 38:12.)

4. *Harshness, crudeness, and insensitivity.* Though not mentioned specifically in the Book of Mormon as obstacles to charity, these vices do much to deaden mankind to things of worth. It is not just the blatant immorality on the screen, in books, and in the lyrics of modern music that prove to be soul-destroying. Man's inhumanity to man in the form of bitter sarcasm, perpetual insults, and the increasing fascination with brutality and violence—all these work upon the heart and mind to desensitize people to people, as well as to those sweet feelings of tenderness and gentility that encourage and evidence love. Whenever the crude, the rough, or the harsh characterize language and interpersonal relations in any given culture, then the people of that culture are on

the high road to destruction: they are offending and alienating the Spirit of the Lord. The Book of Mormon prophets stress again and again that hardened hearts are simply unable to perceive and then receive the quiet whisperings of the Spirit. (2 Nephi 33:2; Alma 13:4; 40:13.) In time what love they do have will be lost, and their crudeness will be transformed and translated into perversion and murder. They shall become like the Nephites who, within four centuries after the coming of Christ, were described by Mormon as being "without civilization," "without order and without mercy," "without principle, and past feeling." (Moroni 9:11, 18, 20.) "For the Spirit of the Lord will not always strive with man. And when the Spirit ceaseth to strive with man then cometh speedy destruction." (2 Nephi 26:11; compare Helaman 13:8; Ether 2:15.)

Charity as a Fruit of the Spirit

Charity is a gift of the Spirit. It is bestowed by God. One does not "work on" one's charity any more than one might work on one's prophecy, dreams, visions, or discernment. Charity is that "more excellent way" (1 Corinthians 12:31) that comes by and through the Holy Ghost as one of the gifts of God. It is true that we have a responsibility to give of ourselves in service to others as a part of our covenantal obligation as Christians. (See Mosiah 18:8–10; James 2:8.) It is true that service is essential to salvation. But service and charity are not necessarily the same. Charity is "the highest, noblest, strongest kind of love, not merely affection; the pure love of Christ. It is never used to denote alms or deeds or benevolence, although it may be a prompting motive." (LDS Bible Dictionary, p. 632.) That is, charity is that gift of the Spirit which motivates us to greater goodness, specifically, greater service and compassion for others. In a manner of speaking, we can serve people without loving them; we cannot truly love them, as the Lord does, without serving them. Bruce C. Hafen has written: "Our own internally generated compassion for the needs of others is a crucial indication of our desire to be followers of the Savior. . . . For that reason, we must be reaching out to others even as we reach out to God, rather than waiting to respond to others' needs until our charitable instincts are quickened by the Spirit. But even then, charity in its full-blown sense is '*bestowed* upon' Christ's righteous followers. Its source, like all other blessings of the Atonement, is the grace of God." (*The Broken Heart,* pp. 195–96; italics in original.)

When Benjamin challenged his people, and us, to be spiritually reborn, to put off the natural man and become a saint through the atonement of Christ, he further instructed us to become as little children—"submissive, meek, humble, patient, *full of love,* willing to submit to all things which the Lord seeth fit to inflict" upon us. (Mosiah 3:19; italics added.) Likewise, Alma warned the people of Ammonihah against procrastination: "But that ye would humble yourselves before the Lord, and call on his holy name, and watch and pray continually, that ye may not be tempted above that which ye can bear, *and thus be led by the Holy Spirit, becoming humble, meek, submissive, patient, full of love and all long-suffering;* having faith on the Lord; having a hope that ye shall receive eternal life; *having the love of God always in your hearts,* that ye may be lifted up at the last day and enter into his rest." (Alma 13:28; italics added.)

Mormon provides the clearest scriptural statement about how to acquire this gift we call charity. "Wherefore, my beloved brethren," he writes, "*pray unto the Father with all the energy of heart, that ye may be filled with this love,* which he hath bestowed upon all who are true followers of his Son, Jesus Christ; that ye may become the sons of God; that when he shall appear we shall be like him, for we shall see him as he is; that we may have this hope; that we may be purified even as he is pure." (Moroni 7:48; italics added.) We see from this profound pronouncement, then, that the purpose of charity is not just to motivate us to Christian service (as important as such is) but also to sanctify us from sin and prepare us not only to be with God but to be like him. (See Ether 12:34.) In Mormon's words, those who become sons and daughters of Jesus Christ—who have applied the atoning blood of the Savior and have been born again as to the things of righteousness—are the ones upon whom the Lord bestows this gift. Bruce Hafen thus explained:

"The ultimate purpose of the gospel of Jesus Christ is to cause the sons and daughters of God to become as Christ is. Those who see religious purpose only in terms of ethical service in the relationship between man and fellowmen may miss that divinely ordained possibility. It is quite possible to render charitable—even 'Christian'—service without developing deeply ingrained and permanent Christlike character. Paul understood this when he warned against giving all one's goods to feed the poor without true charity. . . . We can give without loving, but we cannot love without giving. If our vertical relationship with God is complete, then, by the fruit of that relationship, the horizontal relationship with our fellow beings will also be complete. We then act charitably toward others, not merely because we think we should, but because that is the way we are.

"Service to others will surely bring us closer to God, especially when motivated by an unselfish sense of personal compassion. But even such desirable service will not of itself complete our relationship with God, because it will not by itself result in the bestowal of the complete attributes of godliness. That bestowal requires the ordinances and doctrines of the restored gospel and all the other elements of sacrifice and obedience spelled out in the scriptures. For that reason, while religious philosophies whose highest aim is social relevance may do much good, they will not ultimately lead people to achieve the highest religious purpose, which is to become as God and Christ are." (*The Broken Heart*, pp. 196–97.)

President George Q. Cannon spoke of the failure of the Latter-day Saints to seek after the fruits and the gifts of the Spirit: "We find, even among those who have embraced the Gospel, hearts of unbelief. How many of you, my brethren and sisters, are seeking for these gifts that God has promised to bestow? How many of you, when you bow before your Heavenly Father in your family circle or in your secret places, contend for these gifts to be bestowed upon you? How many of you ask the Father, in the name of Jesus, to manifest Himself to you through these powers and these gifts? Or do you go along day by day like a door turning on its hinges, without having any feeling upon the subject, without exercising any faith whatever; content to be baptized and be members of the Church, and to rest there, thinking that your salvation is secure because you have done this? I say to you, in the name of the Lord, as one of His servants, that you have need to repent of this. You have need to repent of your hardness of heart, of your indifference, and of your carelessness. There is not that diligence, there is not that faith, there is not that seeking for the power of God that there should be among a people who have received the precious promises we have. . . . I say to you that it is our duty to avail ourselves of the privileges which God has placed within our reach. . . .

"I feel to bear testimony to you, my brethren and sisters, . . . that God is the same to-day as He was yesterday; that God is willing to bestow these gifts upon His children. . . . If any of us are imperfect, it is our duty to pray for the gift that will make us perfect. *Have I imperfections? I am full of them. What is my duty? To pray to God to give me the gifts that will correct these imperfections. If I am an angry man, it is my duty to pray for charity, which suffereth long and is kind. Am I an envious man? It is my duty to seek for charity, which envieth not. So with all the gifts of the Gospel.* They are intended for this purpose. No man ought to say, 'Oh, I cannot help this; it is my nature.' He is not justified in it, for the reason that God has promised to give strength to correct these things, and to give gifts that will eradicate them. If a man lack wisdom, it is his duty to ask God for wisdom. The same with everything else. That is the design of God concerning His Church. He wants His Saints to be perfected in the truth. For this purpose He gives these gifts, and bestows them upon those who seek after them, in order that they may be a perfect people upon the face of the earth, notwithstanding their many weaknesses, because God has promised to give the gifts that are necessary for their perfection." (*Millennial Star,* 23 Apr. 1894, pp. 259–61; italics added.)

The Spirit of God sanctifies—it cleanses and purges the human heart. The Spirit does far more, however, than remove uncleanness. It also fills. It fills one with a holy element, with a sacred presence that motivates to a godly walk and goodly works. Such persons filled with the Holy Ghost (and with charity) do not necessarily plan out how they will perform the works of righteousness; they do not always plot and design which deeds and what actions are to be done in every situation. Rather, they embody righteousness. They are goodness. Good works flow from a regenerate heart and evidence their commitment to their Lord and Master. Yes, these persons do have agency. Indeed, they are free, because they have given themselves up to the Lord and his purposes. They choose to do good, but their choices are motivated by the Spirit of the Lord. They live in a world of turmoil but are at peace. They may exist in a society that is steeped in anxiety and uncertainty, but they are at rest. They may live among persons on all sides who are frightened, but they are secure, for charity, or perfect love, casts out all fear. (Moroni 8:16; 1 John 4:18.)

So where do we go from here? We have discussed the ideal. We have seen that the prophets and the Lord challenge us to see to it that our labors are motivated by the pure love of Christ. But what do we do if for the time being our motives for service are less than the highest? Of course we are to strive to do what is right, even if our hearts have not been fully changed. Of course we are to do our home and visiting teaching, even if our motivation for now is more inspection than divine expectation and spontaneous service. Saints cannot remain stagnant. They cannot sit idly by while others perform the labors of the kingdom. They certainly are not justified in doing wrong because they are as yet unregenerated. At the same time, our task is to seek regularly and consistently for that Spirit which gives life and light and which gives substance and consequence to our deeds. Our assignment is not to run faster than we have strength, to labor harder than we have means, or to be truer than true. Our zeal for righteousness must always be tempered and appropriate and accompanied with wisdom. Zion is established in process of time (see Moses 7:21), and, with but few exceptions, the pure in heart become so in like manner. In short, we do the work of the kingdom, but we pray constantly for a purification of our motives and a sanctification of our desires.

Charity as a Key to Enduring to the End

The apostle Peter taught that charity prevents a multitude of sins. (See JST 1 Peter 4:8.) It is not just that one filled with charity is too busy to sin. Rather, the possession of charity is an evidence of the presence and enduring influence of the Holy Ghost, that moral monitor given by the Father to warn, reprove, correct, prick, sanctify, encourage, and comfort. Mormon taught that charity provides the spiritual strength and fortitude which enable one to endure faithfully to the end. "The first fruits of repentance is baptism," he taught; "and baptism cometh by faith unto the fulfilling the commandments; and the fulfilling the commandments bringeth remission of sins; and the remission of sins bringeth meekness, and lowliness of heart; and because of meekness and lowliness of heart cometh *the visitation of the Holy Ghost, which Comforter filleth with hope and perfect love, which love endureth by diligence unto prayer, until the end shall come, when all the saints shall dwell with God.*" (Moroni 8:25–26; italics added.) Stated simply, remission of sins brings the influence of the Comforter, which in turn brings the gifts of the Spirit, preeminent among which is the gift of charity. And charity enables us to endure faithfully to the end. Perhaps this is what Joseph Smith meant when he said: "Until we have perfect love we are liable to fall and when we have a testimony that our names are sealed in the Lamb's book of life we have perfect love and then it is impossible for false Christs to deceive us." (*Teachings of the Prophet Joseph Smith*, p. 9.) Those who possess charity are less prone to have their heads turned by the allurements of a fallen world, less willing to loosen their grasp of the iron rod, on things of enduring worth, to embrace the trappings of Babylon.

There are but few things upon which we may depend with absolute assurance. Elder Jeffrey R. Holland observed: "Life has its share of some fear and some failure. Sometimes things fall short, don't quite measure up. Sometimes in both personal and public life, we are seemingly left without strength to go on. Sometimes people fail us, or economies and circumstance fail us, and life with its hardship and heartache can leave us feeling very alone.

"But when such difficult moments come to us, I testify that there is one thing which will never, ever fail us. One thing alone will stand the test of all time, of all tribulation, all trouble, and all transgression. One thing only never faileth—and that is the pure love of Christ . . . 'If ye have not charity, ye are nothing' (Moroni 7:46). Only the pure love of Christ will see us through. It is Christ's love which suffereth long, and is kind. It is Christ's love which is not puffed up nor easily provoked. Only his pure love enables him—and us—to bear all things, believe all things, hope all things, and endure all things (see Moroni 7:45)." (In Conference Report, Oct. 1989, pp. 32–33.)

Indeed, as Mormon and Paul wrote, charity endures forever. It never fails. (See Moroni 7:46–47; 1 Corinthians 13:8.) Though there may come a day when such gifts of the Spirit as prophecy or tongues or knowledge will have served their useful function, charity—the pure love of Christ—will still be in operation, burning brightly in the hearts and souls of the sons and daughters of Almighty God. "When that which is perfect is come" (1 Corinthians 13:10), the true followers of Jesus Christ will have become like unto him who is the embodiment of love. They will be filled with charity, which is everlasting love. (See Moroni 8:17.)

I have come to believe that the Lord's barometer of righteousness is the heart. No matter the depth of our knowledge, the efficiency of our administration, the charisma with which we influence and lead people — no matter how well we *do* what we do, of much greater significance in the eternal scheme of things is who we are and what we feel toward God and toward our fellow man. It is so easy to be distracted from what matters most, to focus on things — on goals, on excellence programs, on statistics — when in reality it is people that count. I am convinced that people are more important than goals, more important than private or corporative endeavors. People are more important than the attainment of some form of success. God is in the business of people. And so must we be.

In summary, we do not come to love as the Lord loves merely because we work hard at it. True it is we must serve others, that we must concern ourselves with others' needs more than with our own. And true it is that the disciple is expected to bear the burdens and take up the cross of Christian fellowship. But that service and outreach cannot have lasting effect, nor can it result in quiet peace and rest in the giver, unless and until it is motivated from on high. We come to know the cleansing and regenerating power of our Savior only through acknowledging our fallen nature, calling upon him who is mighty to save, and, in the language of the Book of Mormon prophets, relying wholly upon his merits and mercy and grace. (See 2 Nephi 2:8; 31:19; Moroni 6:4.) That forgiveness which comes from Christ evidences and conveys his perfect love, and, in process of time, empowers us to love in like manner. We must pray for forgiveness, for cleansing, for reconciliation with the Father through the Son. And we must pray for charity. We must plead for it. We must ask with all the energy of heart to be so endowed. As we do so, there will come moments of surpassing import, sublime moments that matter, moments in which our whole souls seem to reach out to others with a kind of fellowship and affection that we would not otherwise know.

I have felt that love. I have tasted of its sweet fruit. It is beyond anything earthly, above and beyond anything that mortal man can explain or produce. One of the greatest regrets of my life is that such moments do not come with the regularity and frequency that I would desire. Such love settles the hearts of individuals. It provides moral courage to those who must face difficult challenges. It unites and seals husbands, wives, and children and grants them a foretaste of eternal life. It welds quorums and classes and wards and stakes into a union that is the foundation for that "highest order of priesthood society" we know as Zion. (Spencer W. Kimball, in Conference Report, Oct. 1977, p. 125; compare 4 Nephi 1:15.) And, once again, it comes from that Lord who is the Source of all that is godlike. To the degree that we trust in that Lord and yield our hearts unto him (Helaman 3:35), "I am persuaded," with the apostle Paul, "that neither death, nor life, nor angels, nor principalities, nor powers, nor things present, nor things to come, nor height, nor depth, nor any other creature, shall be able to separate us from the love of God, which is in Christ Jesus our Lord" (Romans 8:38–39).

Chapter Five

Relying upon the Merits, Mercy, and Grace of Christ

What a person trusts in, what he or she relies on — these things are excellent indicators of spiritual maturity. Like the infant that grasps and clings to objects with selfish immaturity, we are so prone to be stingy with our lives, to insist on doing things our way, to chart a course that we want to pursue, to demand complete control. While we labor in this tabernacle of flesh we are subject to a kind of mortal myopia, a tragic shortsightedness in regard to eternal things. In our heart of hearts we know that God's ways are higher than ours and his thoughts and judgment so much grander than our own (Isaiah 55:8–9). Joseph Smith wrote from the Liberty Jail: "The things of God are of deep import; and time, and experience, and careful and ponderous and solemn thoughts can only find them out. Thy mind, O man! if thou wilt lead a soul unto salvation [in this case, our own], must stretch as high as the utmost heavens, and search into and contemplate the darkest abyss, and the broad expanse of eternity — thou must commune with God. How much more dignified and noble are the thoughts of God, than the vain imaginations of the human

heart! None but fools will trifle with the souls of men."
(*Teachings of the Prophet Joseph Smith,* p. 137.)

We know, deep down, that the wise course is to allow the
Captain of our soul to have sway, that he can make us into
new creatures far beyond anything we might bring about in
our own unillumined and unassisted manner. In the words
of President Ezra Taft Benson, "Men and women who turn
their lives over to God will discover that He can make a lot
more out of their lives than they can. He will deepen their
joys, expand their vision, quicken their minds, strengthen
their muscles, lift their spirits, multiply their blessings, increase their opportunities, comfort their souls, raise up
friends, and pour out peace." (*Teachings of Ezra Taft Benson,*
p. 361.) It is through the atoning grace of Christ that we are
liberated from skewed perceptions, through the transforming
powers of the Holy One of Israel that we become holy and
thus able to see things as they really are. As we reach up to
grasp the hand of him who has all things in his power, we
thereby tighten our grasp on eternal life; we begin the process
of spiritual growth.

Fighting Feelings of Failure

At the beginning of a presidency meeting some years ago,
the stake president read a letter from a young woman in one
of the wards. I knew her very well because I had served for
a time as her bishop. She and her husband were the parents
of three beautiful little girls. The mother, whom I will here
call Brenda, was active and involved and into everything; she
worked faithfully in the Young Women's program, was always
the life of ward parties, and sought out every opportunity
to contribute to parent-teacher functions, civic issues, and

community affairs. "Go, go, go" was her motto. The stake president read the letter, which said simply:

"Dear President:

"I want to do everything the Lord has asked me to do. I want to do everything the Church has asked me to do. In order to do so, I decided to make a list of the things that I have been asked to do in the Church during the last six months. A copy of the list is enclosed." Then followed about three pages of items that had been required of her. It was quite an imposing list. She closed as follows: "I have only one question — HOW?" And then she signed the letter: "Dejectedly, Brenda."

The president turned to the other counselor and asked: "Jack, isn't that unfortunate?" Jack nodded soberly. Then the president turned to me: "Bob," he said, "does this letter get to your heart the way it gets to mine?" I answered that it surely did. "Good," he responded, "because I want you to deal with it." "What would you like me to do?" I asked with a gulp. "Just meet with her for a few minutes and see if you can help her." I agreed and made the appointment. What I thought would be a brief pep talk really turned out to be a rather lengthy meeting. I listened as Brenda poured out her concerns for over two hours. It was a very intense occasion filled with much emotion. If I were to summarize what she said in one sentence — a sentence, by the way, with which she concluded her expression — it would go something like this: "I can't do it all. I can't be the perfect mother, the perfect wife, the perfect Church leader, the perfect citizen. I'm tired. In fact, I'm worn out. I tell you, I just can't do it all!"

I startled her a bit when I said, "I know. I can't either." Brenda looked at me with suspicion. "You admit that?" she asked. "I admit that," I came back. She followed up: "Would you admit it in public, perhaps in a stake conference, some-time?" I thought for a second and said, "Yes, I would be pleased to talk about it in a stake conference." (By the way, I did address this matter in my stake conference talk a few months later.) She then asked, "How do you deal with the guilt?" My response surprised her again: "I don't have any, at least not over all the things I just can't do yet." I think she left our meeting with a different view of things; she seemed to be at peace.

Let me relate a second instance, one involving a sixteen-year-old young woman we'll call Sarah. Sarah became aware that she had very uncomfortable and unkind feelings toward a member of her Laurel class. She had been raised in the Church, had been active and involved all her young life, and was well taught. She determined upon a plan to solve her problem. She would get up an hour earlier each morning and stay up an hour later each night reading the Book of Mormon. This she did religiously for three months. At the end of that time Sarah discovered (to her surprise and disappointment) that she still harbored unkind feelings toward the other young woman. "Well," she concluded, "if that doesn't work, then I'll multiply my efforts. I'll get up two hours earlier in the morning and stay up two hours later at night reading the Book of Mormon; I'll fast at least two times a week; and I'll volunteer my services at the temple once per week." At the end of six months Sarah realized that she had read the Book of Mormon through twice; had lost a good deal of weight; and, sadly, still had unkind feelings toward the other young woman. She cried out, "Why? Why? If this is the true Church, why doesn't my hard work count? Why can't I solve my prob-lems?"

Why, indeed? Why wouldn't Sarah's problems be solved

through her superhuman effort? Why would Brenda, and a thousand others like Brenda, labor in guilt over all the things she couldn't get around to? Though each of us is different and has unique challenges and strengths, there is one problem to which most of us are susceptible, one which keeps us from enjoying the kind of peace and comfort that the Saints of the Most High ought to—and have a right to—enjoy. I fear that one reason we have feelings such as Brenda and Sarah had—feelings that we just don't measure up, feelings that no matter how much we do it isn't enough—is our failure to trust in the Lord and rely on him. We live in a culture in which excellence and success and victory are drilled into us from the time we are old enough to take part in society. Words such as *submission* and *surrender* are almost foreign to our way of life. But in fact submission is absolutely necessary if we are to be happy; surrender is vital if we are to be at peace. Christ invites his disciples to submit to him, to have an eye single to his glory, to yield their hearts unto him. Christ invites his disciples to surrender, to lay down their mortal weapons and acknowledge his lordship. As we are able to trust in the Master—to trust in his time frame, his way of life, his vision of what is best for us—we begin to mature in our faith.

Without such trust in the Lord, without relinquishing our own stranglehold on life, we will probably either work ourselves into a frenzy of spiritual and physical exhaustion, or else find ourselves doing all the right things but feeling little pleasure in doing so. In short, we may find ourselves "going through the motions." One writer used the following story to illustrate this matter of going through the motions: "Imagine yourself in a large house, in which are living both deaf and hearing people. They are all mixed together, and you can't tell by looking who is deaf and who has hearing. Sitting in a room by himself is a man. As you watch, you notice that he is tapping his toes rhythmically and snapping his fingers in time. You know what is happening. He's listening to music, and obviously enjoying himself. His whole body wants to respond to what his ears are receiving. There's nothing strange or mysterious about it.

"But now, let's add a new person to the scene. One of the deaf persons opens the door and enters the room. He immediately sees the first man and walks over to him and smiles a greeting. The deaf man watches the music-lover for a few moments. 'He sure seems to be enjoying himself,' he thinks. 'I think I'll try it, too.' So the deaf man sits next to the first man and begins to imitate him. Awkwardly and haltingly at first, he tries to snap his fingers, tap his toes, and move like the person next to him. Everybody has some sense of rhythm, whether they can hear or not. After a little practice, the deaf man is snapping and tapping in time with the first man. He even smiles a little and shrugs· 'It's not *that* much fun,' he thinks, 'but it's okay.'

"Let's now add our final factor to the story. A third man walks into the room. What does he see? *Two men, apparently doing the same thing.* But is there a difference? Absolutely! All the difference in the world! The first man's actions are natural *responses* to the music he hears. The deaf man is only *imitating* those outward actions—even though he can't hear a note." (Bob George, *Classic Christianity,* pp. 152–53, italics in original.)

So often we end up going through the motions—performing the appropriate labors but not enjoying it, doing the right things but having to grit our teeth and force ourselves to do them—because we are trying to do good works against a fallen and unregenerate nature. Don't get me wrong—it's always better to do the right thing, even for the wrong reason, than to do the wrong thing. I hear people say: "It would be better to stay home from church than to go to church, given the way I feel!" Not really. It's better to go to church. There is a better and higher motivation, however, one that is above and beyond self-discipline, well beyond sheer willpower and dogged determination. It is a motivation borne of the Spirit, one that comes to us as a result of a change of heart.

For years, it seems to me, many Latter-day Saints have refused to speak or teach or believe much about the principle or doctrine of salvation by grace because we did not want to be confused with others in the Christian world who believe in salvation by grace *alone.* That is illustrated quite well in an experience I had. Before leaving on a mission, I approached one of my priesthood leaders with the question, "What does it mean to be saved by grace?" Having been raised in the southern states and the Bible Belt, I had heard the phrase many times from numerous friends. My priesthood leader—a powerful preacher of the gospel and one who knew the doctrines well—responded quickly: "We don't believe in that." I asked further, "We don't believe in salvation by grace? Why not?" His comeback: "Because the Baptists do!"

His answer speaks volumes. If the Protestants are on the far right in regard to this matter of grace, then we just have to be on the far left. The problem with this reasoning, of course, is that by such prejudice we may miss something, miss and thus fail to grasp and experience the essential verity so vital to a dynamic faith in Jesus Christ.

Because ours is a day of intense involvement, perpetual motion, and constant change and complexity, many of us, like Brenda, who wanted to be a perfect wife and mother, a perfect homemaker, a perfect Mia Maid adviser, and a perfect citizen in the community, are stretched to the limit. Further, many have recognized their limits, become aware of what is left to do, acknowledged the gap between the two (between the ideal and the reality), and thrown in the towel: they've surrendered to the spirit of discouragement. For another thing, repeated claims of Christian groups around the world that Latter-day Saints are not Christian, that we are not entitled to the name and designation of the Savior, have caused us to search and delve into the core doctrines of scripture. Many Mormons have found themselves reading the scriptures (ancient and modern) with an intensity and a fervor that they have not known before, not only to sustain and defend the faith against carpers and critics but also to come to know their religion for themselves. In that regard, I am convinced that one of the reasons we find ourselves reflecting on the matter of grace more today than we did twenty years ago is that we have rediscovered the Book of Mormon. The Book of Mormon teaches the doctrine of Christ — including the Creation, the Fall, the Atonement, and the need for absolute reliance on the Savior — more clearly than any other scriptural record we have. Relying upon the merits and mercy and grace of the Holy Messiah is the burden of that sacred volume. President Ezra Taft Benson's call to the Church to search, study, and apply the teachings of the Book of Mormon will surely prove to be a message that will have everlasting influence on the members of the Restored Church.

The New Life in Christ

As we begin to mature spiritually, as we begin the process of becoming steadfast and immovable, we come to realize that some things simply matter more than others. Some topics of discussion, even those that are intellectually stimulating, must take a backseat to more basic and fundamental truths. That is the case with regard to what the scriptures call the gospel or the doctrine of Christ, those foundational verities associated with the person and powers of Jesus Christ, the Savior and Redeemer. Who he is, what he has done for us, and how we may appropriate those transforming powers in our own lives are paramount and central issues; all else, however supplementary, is secondary. Joseph Smith the Prophet thus observed that "the fundamental principles of our religion are the testimony of the Apostles and Prophets, concerning Jesus Christ, that He died, was buried, and rose again the third day, and ascended into heaven; and all other things which pertain to our religion are only appendages to it." (*Teachings of the Prophet Joseph Smith,* p. 121.)

We speak much about our appreciation for the gospel of Jesus Christ. We bear testimony of the gospel. And what is it that we testify of? Joseph Smith wrote: "And this is the gospel, *the glad tidings, . . . that he came into the world, even Jesus, to be crucified for the world, and to bear the sins of the world, and to sanctify the world, and to cleanse it from all unrighteousness;* that through him all might be saved whom the Father had put into his power and made by him." (D&C 76:40–42; italics added; compare 3 Nephi 27:13–14.) When we bear witness that we know the gospel is true, we are testifying that Jesus is the Christ, that death and hell and endless torment have been overcome through his atoning sacrifice, and that the transformation from fallen creature to spiritual being comes to pass through the redeeming power of his blood. Power unto life and salvation is in a Person, the person of Jesus Christ. We may know much about the Church and kingdom of God, all of which is very important, but if we are not anchored to the truth of the gospel, we will not enjoy the blessings that might otherwise be ours. Elder Boyd K. Packer thus observed: "Truth, glorious truth, proclaims there is . . . a Mediator. . . . Through Him mercy can be fully extended to each of us without offending the eternal law of justice. *This truth is the very root of Christian doctrine. You may know much about the gospel as it branches out from there, but if you only know the branches and those branches do not touch that root, if they have been cut free from that truth, there will be no life nor substance nor redemption in them.*" (In Conference Report, Apr. 1977, p. 80; italics added.)

As inspired as programs or policies or procedures are, as successful as organizations and auxiliaries may prove to be, it is Christ that saves, Christ that changes the human heart, Christ that binds up the broken heart. Abinadi, in censuring the priests of the wicked King Noah, said: "And now ye have said that salvation cometh by the law of Moses. I say unto you that it is expedient that ye should keep the law of Moses as yet; but I say unto you, that the time shall come when it shall no more be expedient to keep the law of Moses. And moreover, I say unto you, that salvation doth not come by the law alone; and were it not for the atonement, which God himself shall make for the sins and iniquities of his people, that they must unavoidably perish, notwithstanding the law of Moses." (Mosiah 13:27–28.) In applying these ancient words to our own day, Elder Bruce R. McConkie pointed out: "Suppose we have the scriptures, the gospel, the priest-hood, the Church, the ordinances, the organization, even the keys of the kingdom—everything that now is down to the last jot and tittle—and yet there is no atonement of Christ. What then? Can we be saved? Will all our good works save us? Will we be rewarded for all our righteousness?

"Most assuredly we will not. We are not saved by works

alone, no matter how good; we are saved because God sent his Son to shed his blood in Gethsemane and on Calvary that all through him might ransomed be. We are saved by the blood of Christ.

"To paraphrase Abinadi: 'Salvation doth not come by the Church alone: and were it not for the atonement, given by the grace of God as a free gift, all men must unavoidably perish, and this notwithstanding the Church and all that appertains to it.' " ("What Think Ye of Salvation by Grace?" *Brigham Young University Fireside and Devotional Speeches,* 1983–84, p. 48.)

With all of this in mind, with a clear picture of the fact that it is Christ that can and does make the difference in human souls, we need to focus on a dimension of his atoning mission that often receives too little treatment. As important as it is to know that Jesus *died* for us, it is equally important to stress that we have not begun to fully enjoy the blessings of the Atonement until he comes to *live* in us. To say this another way, we need to focus upon Christ's *life-sharing* as much as we focus upon his life-giving. Paul explained in his epistle to the Galatians: "I am crucified with Christ: nevertheless *I live; yet not I, but Christ liveth in me.*" (Galatians 2:20; italics added.) But how can such be? How can a resurrected, exalted, immortal being live in us? It is by the power of his Spirit, the Holy Ghost.

The Holy Ghost is the Revelator. He is the Comforter. And he is the Sanctifier. As Sanctifier, it is his task to work upon the hearts of those who repent and offer themselves a living sacrifice unto Christ; it is by the Holy Ghost that people are cleansed and purified, the means by which they have dross and filth burned out of their souls as though by fire. But the Holy Ghost does more than cleanse. He *fills.* He fills us with a holy element that motivates to a godly walk and goodly works. "The process of canning," one Christian thinker has observed, "is an excellent illustration of the two parts of the gospel. Let's say that you are going to preserve some peaches. What is the first thing you have to do? Sterilize the jars. Why the process of *sterilization?* So that the contents of the jars—the peaches—will be preserved from spoiling.

"Imagine a husband coming home and finding his wife boiling jars in the kitchen. 'What are you doing, honey?'

" 'Sterilizing jars.'

" 'Why are you doing that?' the husband asks.

" 'I just like clean jars,' she answers.

"The husband is clearly at a loss. 'What are you going to do next?' he asks.

" 'Keep them clean!'

"This story doesn't make much sense, does it? You have never seen anyone decorate his kitchen with a sterile jar collection. No, the only reason to sterilize jars is *because you intend to put something in them.* We would never expect to find a person involved in only half the process of canning, just cleansing jars. But we have done this exact thing with the gospel!" In fact, one more step is essential, one with which Latter-day Saints can identify quite well. "As a matter of fact, there is one final part of the canning process. After sterilizing the jars and filling them with fruit, the jars are *sealed.* Sealing keeps the good things inside and the bad things that would spoil the contents outside." (George, *Classic Christianity,* pp. 62, 63; italics in original.)

The apostle Paul asked the Roman Saints: "Know ye not, that so many of us as were baptized into Jesus Christ were baptized into his death? Therefore we are buried with him by baptism into death: that like as Christ was raised up from the dead by the glory of the Father, even so we also should walk in newness of life." (Romans 6:3–4.) This scripture has reference to the newness of life that can be ours in mortality through the redeeming powers of Christ. As the Spirit begins to work in us we, in process of time, begin to be born again or be born from above. The life of Christ begins to be manifest in us. We have his image in our countenances. (Alma 5:14.) Ours is a godly walk and conversation. (D&C 20:69.) Our behavior begins to reflect our belief wherever we may be — on the highways, at the ballparks, in the gymnasiums, or in the supermarkets. Our tongue and our actions betray us as Christians.

Jesus came to earth on his search and rescue mission not only to change us but also to exchange with us. In short, as we agree to accept him as our Mediator and spiritual Benefactor, as we take his name upon us and strive by covenant to live a life befitting a disciple of Christ, he agrees to justify us, meaning to exonerate us or pronounce us innocent. As we fully come unto Christ—with no desire to hold back or to hold on to the things of the world—he takes our sins and then imputes to us his righteousness. What a marvelous exchange! Paul taught: "I count all things but loss for the excellency of the knowledge of Christ Jesus my Lord: for whom I have suffered the loss of all things, and do count them but dung, that I may win Christ, and be found in him, *not having mine own righteousness, which is of the law, but that which is through the faith of Christ, the righteousness which is of God by faith.*" (Philippians 3:8–9; italics added.) Likewise, to the Corinthians he delivered a witness of the Master's exchange: "Therefore if any man be in Christ, he is a new creature: old things are passed away; behold, all things are become new. And all things are of God, who hath reconciled us to himself

by Jesus Christ, and hath given to us the ministry of reconciliation. . . . Now then we are ambassadors for Christ, as
though God did beseech you by us: we pray you in Christ's
stead, be ye reconciled to God. For *he [the Father] hath made
him [the Son] to be sin for us, who knew no sin; that we might
be made the righteousness of God in him.*" (2 Corinthians 5:17–
18, 20–21; italics added.)

Some people complain that it is hard to live the gospel,
to abide by all the standards of the Church. From one perspective, it is not hard to live the gospel unless we are trying
to hold on to Babylon and the ways of the world. (See Robert
L. Millet, *An Eye Single to the Glory of God,* chap. 1.) From
another perspective, it isn't hard: it's impossible! At least it's
impossible if we try to keep all the rules and obey all the
statutes on our own, without divine assistance. Just as Brenda
explained, we can't do it all. And here we come face to face
with the matter of works. How do I do all the works expected
of me? How do I perform the tasks assigned to me? Simply
stated, I cannot do it all on my own. Paul explained: "For by
grace are ye saved through faith; and that not of yourselves:
it is the gift of God: not of works, lest any man should boast.
For *we are his workmanship, created in Christ Jesus unto good
works,* which God hath before ordained that we should walk
in them." (Ephesians 2:8–10; italics added.) In a scripture
that Latter-day Saints are prone to quote when confronted
by certain Christians who cite the above passage from Ephesians, Paul taught: "Wherefore, my beloved, as ye have always
obeyed, not as in my presence only, but now much more in
my absence, *work out your own salvation* with fear and trem-
bling." (Philippians 2:12; italics added.) And there it is—the
commission to work out our salvation by ourselves. But not
so fast. The next verse is quite instructive: "For *it is God*

which worketh in you both to will and to do of his good pleasure." (Philippians 2:13; italics added.)

Are works unimportant, then? Doesn't it matter what we
do? Of course works matter. Of course it matters what we
do. But the scriptures attest again and again that it is not our
works that save us. Our works—our reception of the ordinances of salvation, our acts of goodness and benevolence,
our contribution to the work of the kingdom—are necessary,
but insufficient. As Elder McConkie pointed out, our
works, no matter how many or how good, are not enough.
We are not saved by our works. Some people say that we are
saved by the grace of Christ but exalted by our works. That
also is false. Our works evidence our faith in Christ and our
desire to follow him and rely upon his atoning grace. But
there are simply not enough loaves of bread to bake or home
teaching visits to make or meetings to attend to save me from
the woes of sin; such requires the mediation of a God. The
strangest matter of all is that it is *his* works—the works of
Christ—that save us. Thus Lehi declared to Jacob: "Wherefore, I know that thou art redeemed, *because of the righteousness of thy Redeemer.*" Indeed, as Lehi went on to say, "There
is no flesh that can dwell in the presence of God, save it be
through the merits, and mercy, and grace of the Holy Messiah." (2 Nephi 2:3, 8; italics added; compare Alma 22:14.)

The issue is not whether we are saved by grace or works.
That is the wrong question, one that has alienated people for
too long. It is, as C. S. Lewis observed, "like asking which
blade in a pair of scissors is most necessary." (*Mere Christianity,* p. 129.) The real questions to be asked are, In whom do
I trust? On whom do I rely? Do I trust in my works? Do I
rely on my goodness? "And now, my beloved brethren,"
Nephi proclaimed in a discussion of the doctrine of Christ,

"after ye have gotten into this strait and narrow path, I would ask if all is done? Behold, I say unto you, Nay; for ye have not come thus far save it were by the word of Christ with unshaken faith in him, *relying wholly upon the merits of him who is mighty to save.*" (2 Nephi 31:19; italics added.) Wholly means absolutely, completely, perfectly. Is this not the same message that Moroni delivered when he spoke of the Nephite Church? In speaking of those who had come into the true church and begun the process of spiritual growth, Moroni wrote: "And after they had been received unto baptism, and were wrought upon and cleansed by the power of the Holy Ghost, they were numbered among the people of the church of Christ; and their names were taken, that they might be remembered and nourished by the good word of God, to keep them in the right way, to keep them continually watchful unto prayer, *relying alone upon the merits of Christ,* who was the author and the finisher of their faith." (Moroni 6:4; italics added.)

Imagine that you had been asked to serve as the defense attorney for a man who had been arrested for robbing a local food store. How would you proceed? Well, you think back to all the Perry Mason episodes you have viewed and plot out a defense. First, you need to establish that your client has no motive, that he is financially in good shape, and that to steal a hundred dollars from a food store makes no sense. Then you might work on his access to the crime, that he was nowhere near the scene at the time the crime was committed, that he has an alibi. Finally, you might work on the matter of his reputation. You stress to the jury that this man is the beloved father of nine children, that he is civic-minded, is a little league baseball coach, and an active scouter. In short, such a crime is absolutely foreign to his reputation. Such an approach just might do the trick. Think for a moment, however, of how those in the courtroom might respond to a defense that went something like the following: You stand and speak with much confidence, "Judge, jury, I demand that you set this man free!" The judge answers: "On what grounds?" You reply: "Because of my excellent reputation as an attorney, because of my marvelous record of service to the innocent who are unjustly accused." One can imagine how the judge and jury would respond. You would no doubt be laughed out of the courtroom. And yet, note in a modern revelation how the Savior pleads our case, how he mediates between us and the Eternal Father: "Listen to him who is the advocate with the Father, who is pleading your cause before him — saying: Father, behold the sufferings and death of him who did no sin, in whom thou wast well pleased; behold the blood of thy Son which was shed, the blood of him whom thou gavest that thyself might be glorified." What a strange defense! What an unusual manner of defending us! The Lord here pleads our cause *on the basis of his merits;* we are saved through *his works,* his mercy and grace. And what does he require? "Wherefore, Father, spare these my brethren that believe on my name, that they may come unto me and have everlasting life." (D&C 45:3–5.)

On this matter of trusting the Lord, C. S. Lewis has written: "In one sense, the road back to God is a road of moral effort, of trying harder and harder. But in another sense it is not trying that is ever going to bring us home. All this trying leads up to *the vital moment at which you turn to God and say, 'You must do this, I can't.'* . . . The thing I am talking of now may not happen to every one in a sudden flash — as it did to St. Paul or Bunyan: it may be so gradual that no one could ever point to a particular hour or even a particular year. And what matters is the nature of the change in itself, not how we feel while it is happening. *It is the change from being confident about our own efforts to the state in which we despair of doing anything for ourselves and leave it to God.*

"I know the words 'leave it to God' can be misunderstood, but they must stay for the moment. *The sense in which a Christian leaves it to God is that he puts all his trust in Christ:* trusts that Christ will somehow share with him the perfect human obedience which He carried out from His birth to His crucifixion: *that Christ will make the man more like Himself and, in a sense, make good his deficiencies.* . . . And, in yet another sense, handing everything over to Christ does not, of course, mean that you stop trying. To trust Him means, of course, trying to do all that He says. There would be no sense in saying you trusted a person if you would not take his advice. Thus if you have really handed yourself over to Him, it must follow that you are trying to obey Him. But *trying in a new way, a less worried way."* (*Mere Christianity,* pp. 128–29; italics added.)

The new life in Christ is thus far more than a change in behavior, more than a slight correction of a faulty action or two. It is a renovation of human nature. As one writer has observed, "We may be quite sure that Christ-centredness and Christ-likeness will never be attained by our own unaided efforts. How can self drive out self? As well expect Satan to drive out Satan!" (John Stott, *Life in Christ,* p. 109.) And there is perhaps no better statement on the nature of our change from death to life than that by President Ezra Taft Benson: "The Lord works from the inside out. The world works from the outside in. The world would take people out of the slums. Christ takes the slums out of people, and then they take themselves out of the slums. The world would mold men by changing their environment. Christ changes men, who then change their environment. The world would shape human behavior, but Christ can change human nature." (In Conference Report, Oct. 1985, p. 5.) As we begin to mature spiritually, we may find ourselves praying more earnestly about our nature, about what we *are,* as much as we pray about what we *do.* Indeed, what we do becomes a reflection and an extension of what we are, what we really are.

The Master calls us to perfection. It is a lofty goal, one that too often strikes fear or, more often, discouragement into the hearts of all of us who fall so very short of the ideal. The fact is, no mortal man or woman will achieve moral perfection in this life or will traverse the path of life without some sort of spiritual detour. Jesus alone accomplished that superhuman task. But we can become perfect in eternity, and we are able to do so in this life to the degree that we yield our hearts unto Christ and rely upon his merits, mercy, and grace. The Lord offers hope. He offers peace. He offers rest, all in and through him. Moroni pleaded with us to "come unto Christ, and be perfected in him." (Moroni 10:32.) We are perfected in Christ, in the same way that we are reborn, justified, and sanctified in Christ. We become perfect — that is, whole, complete, fully formed, and finished — as we join with him by covenant. Jesus thus becomes the author and *finisher* of our faith. (See Moroni 6:4; Hebrews 12:2.) Those who go to the celestial kingdom are those who are just men and women who have been *made perfect* "through Jesus the mediator of the new covenant, who wrought out this perfect atonement through the shedding of his own blood." (D&C 76:69.)

Stephen Robinson, my friend and colleague, has given the following excellent analogy:

"Perfection comes through the Atonement of Christ. We become one with him, with a perfect being. And as we become one, there is a merger. Some of my students are studying business, and they understand it better if I talk in business terms. You take a small bankrupt firm that's about ready to go under and merge it with a corporate giant. What happens? Their assets and liabilities flow together, and the new entity that is created is solvent.

"It's like when Janet and I got married. I was overdrawn; Janet had money in the bank. By virtue of making that commitment, of entering into that covenant relationship of marriage with my wife, we became a joint account. No longer was there an I, and no longer a she — now it was *we*. My liabilities and her assets flowed into each other, and for the first time in months I was in the black.

"Spiritually, this is what happens when we enter into the covenant relationship with our Savior. We have liabilities, he has assets. He proposes to us a covenant relationship. I use the word 'propose' on purpose because it is a marriage of a spiritual sort that is being proposed. That is why he is called the Bridegroom. This covenant relationship is so intimate that it can be described as a marriage. I become one with Christ, and as partners we work together for my salvation and my exaltation. My liabilities and his assets flow together into each other. I do all that I can do, and he does what I cannot yet do. The two of us together are perfect." ("Believing Christ," *Brigham Young University Fireside and Devotional Speeches,* 1989–90, pp. 120–21.)

A Risky Doctrine?

As I have addressed this subject in lectures or firesides, there have been occasions when people have responded:

"Wait a minute! Aren't you just a little nervous about teaching these things? Don't you worry that some people will take what you say as license to goof off?" I suppose there is some risk in that regard. The apostle Paul certainly wrestled in his day with Saints who took his words on the liberating power of the gospel as license to sin. People who want an excuse to do little or who seek to rationalize their worst efforts will always latch on to such twisted views. But I think there is a greater risk here. I'm thinking of those people on the other side of this issue, those members of the Church who are doing all they know how to do, good people who push themselves, noble souls who double and triple their efforts after an initial failure, fine and upstanding Latter-day Saints who wrestle constantly with feelings of inadequacy. I worry about them far more. I worry sometimes that if we understate the Atonement, if we see Jesus only as he who forgives gross sin, instead of as the One sent to "bind up the brokenhearted" (Isaiah 61:1), we may not grasp the essential truth that our Lord can and will bring peace of soul to those who are filled with bitterness, hostility, anger, jealousy, fear, loneliness, and feelings of inadequacy.

Several years ago I spoke to a group of Latter-day Saints on the topic of "relying wholly upon the merits of him who is mighty to save." (2 Nephi 31:19.) About three weeks later I received a letter from a woman who had attended the lecture. She wrote to express appreciation for what had been said and to ask for clarification on a few matters. Without disclosing too many personal details, she related to me that hers had been a full and rich life, that she had a wonderful husband and adorable children. She then wrote of her struggles to do all that had been assigned her, to keep up with what she described as a maddening pace, to "perform" against what she believed to be an impossible standard. She said, in essence, that she really did want to do it all. She stated that there was no doubt in her mind that the Church was true and that this was our Father's plan. But then she said: "I'm worn out. I just don't have the strength to go on. What do I do?" I sat on the letter for over a month. I prayed for direction as to how to help her see things in proper perspective. I finally wrote back the following:

"Dear Sister:

"The subject of salvation by grace has been on my mind for a number of years now. I sense deeply that this is one of the major burdens of scripture and one that we as Latter-day Saints would do well to better understand and apply, especially in light of so many who struggle with feelings of frustration, hopelessness, and exhaustion. The following represent just a few thoughts, random reflections on this subject of how to rely more on the Lord, how to get beyond the frame of mind where we feel a constant need to double and redouble our efforts when all does not go as anticipated. They are given as I think of them, in no particular order. They are also my own conclusions, and they really have no higher authority than that. But I feel that they are true.

"1. I believe that the Lord wants us to succeed and that he has every intention of bringing back as many of his children as is possible. Discouragement and despondency are not of the Lord. They are of Lucifer. The arch-deceiver would have us lose our balance, lose track of what matters most in life, and focus too much on the less significant. He would have us labor to exhaustion in secondary causes.

"2. We cannot do everything we are asked to do, at least not in a few weeks or months. It takes some time to be able to figure this out. One of the hardest things to do is to recognize when we are stretching to the limit, and then to stop and slow down.

"3. There are some things about us—personality quirks, deep feelings (jealousies, fears, loneliness, bitterness, etc.)— that we cannot completely change on our own. We can devise and implement all the behavior modification programs possible, can chart and record and recite our flaws till doomsday, and still not overcome them. These require divine assistance, an assistance that may bring about change quickly and dramatically, or, more than likely, a change that will come in process of time. As the Savior explained through Moroni, his grace—his enabling power—is sufficient to change our nature, if we acknowledge his power so to do and then rely on him as the Change Agent. (Ether 12:27.) As C. S. Lewis wrote: 'If . . . what we are matters even more than what we do—if, indeed, what we do matters chiefly as evidence of what we are—then it follows that the change which I most need to undergo is a change that my own direct, voluntary efforts cannot bring about. . . . I cannot, by direct moral effort, give myself new motives. After the first few steps in the Christian life we realise that everything which really needs to be done in our souls can be done only by God.' (*Mere Christianity,* p. 165.)

"4. One way I have come to rely on the Lord more is to pray constantly for a purification of my motives. When I am more concerned with pleasing the Lord than with pleasing others, I am less 'uptight' when my meager efforts do not quite measure up to others' expectations. There is something to be said for doing what you feel and hope is right and then letting the consequence follow.

"5. There is also great virtue in praying that the Lord will let us know our limits, let us know when further labors on our part will in reality be spiritually counterproductive. More and more our prayers become: 'O God, help me know when my offering is acceptable.' When we feel we have reached our limits, our prayers become: 'Heavenly Father, I've done all I know how to do. Please, help me.'

"6. Because we are human—because we are weak and mortal and tired and frail—we will probably never reach the point in this life when we have done 'all we can do.' Too many of us misread 2 Nephi 25:23 and conclude that the Lord can assist us only *after* we have done 'all we can do.' That is incorrect; he can and does help us all along the way. Further, I think Nephi is trying to stress that no matter how much we do, it simply will not be enough to guarantee salvation, without Christ's glorious intervention. Restating Nephi, 'Above and beyond all we can do, it is by the grace of Christ that we are saved.' To push ourselves beyond what is appropriate in our effort to 'work out our salvation' is, in a strange sort of way, a statement that we fear that we must do the job ourselves if we expect it to get done. Don't get me wrong: I know, as do you, that we must do our duty in the Church and that the 'works of righteousness' are necessary. What is so very unnecessary is the type of pharisaical extremism and the subsequent negative feelings that too often characterize the efforts of some members of the Church.

"I have a conviction that God is unquestionably aware of us. He loves you and he loves me. This I know. He certainly wants us to improve, but he definitely does not want us to spend our days languishing in guilt. Rather, the gospel of Jesus Christ is intended to liberate us, to lift and lighten our burdens. If it is not doing that in our personal lives, then I contend that our approach and understanding—not necessarily the quantity of work to be done—may need some adjustment. May the Lord bless you with the assurance of his love and his willingness to bring you peace and rest."

A most entertaining and instructive story on the matter of risk was given by a Protestant minister. In it we see many of the elements that we have spoken of, elements that become a part of our lives as we begin to mature spiritually. "I remember when I first earned my license to drive," Charles Swindoll has written. "I was about sixteen, as I recall. I'd been driving off and on for three years (scary thought, isn't it?). My father had been with me most of the time during my learning experiences, calmly sitting alongside me in the front seat, giving me tips, helping me know what to do. My mother usually wasn't in on those excursions because she spent more of her time biting her nails (and screaming) than she did advising. My father was a little more easygoing. Loud noises and screeching brakes didn't bother him nearly as much. My grandfather was the best of all. When I would drive his car, I would hit things . . . *Boom!* He'd say stuff like, 'Just keep on going, Bud. I can buy more fenders, but I can't buy more grandsons. You're learning.' What a great old gentleman. After three years of all that nonsense, I finally earned my license.

"I'll never forget the day I came in, flashed my newly acquired permit, and said, 'Dad, look!' He goes, 'Whoa! Look at this. You got your license. Good for you!' Holding the keys to his car, he tossed them in my direction and smiled, 'Tell you what, son . . . you can have the car for two hours, all on your own.' Only four words, but how wonderful: 'All on your own.'

"I thanked him, danced out to the garage, opened the car door, and shoved the key into the ignition. My pulse rate must have shot up to 180 as I backed out of the driveway and roared off. While cruising along 'all on my own,' I began to think wild stuff—like, *This car can probably do 100 miles an hour. I could go to Galveston and back twice in two hours if I averaged 100 miles an hour. I can fly down the Gulf Freeway and even run a few lights. After all, nobody's here to say 'Don't!'* We're talking dangerous, crazy thoughts! But you know what? I didn't do any of them. I don't believe I drove above the speed limit. In fact, I distinctly remember turning into the driveway early . . . didn't even stay away the full two hours. Amazing, huh? I had my dad's car all to myself with a full gas tank in a context of total privacy and freedom, but I didn't go crazy. Why? My relationship with my dad and my granddad was so strong that I couldn't, even though I had a license and nobody was in the car to restrain me. Over a period of time there had developed a sense of trust, a deep love relationship that held me in restraint." (*The Grace Awakening,* pp. 47–48; italics in original.)

Trust and reliance on the Lord lead to obedience. The more we trust in him, the more he endows us with his power, his might, and his goodness. He extends to us his grace, meaning a power that enables us to do things we could not do on our own. Our righteousness is then borne of the Spirit, our works are his works, and the deeds we do have a lasting impact on our brothers and sisters and a sanctifying influence on ourselves. On his mighty arm we rely. Because of who he is and what he has done for us, there is no obstacle to eternal life too great to overcome. Because of him, our minds can be at peace. Our souls may rest.

Chapter Six

Building on the Rock of Our Redeemer

Life is too short to spend our days laboring in secondary causes. Nothing could be more frustrating than to devote oneself to a cause that is found in time to be fruitless, to climb a ladder that one eventually discovers to be leaning against the wrong wall. Surely one aspect of maturity is being able to tell the difference, being able to discern the crucial from the convenient, the fundamental from the fleeting. Some things simply matter more than others. Our challenge is to sift through not only the sordid but also the subsidiary and secondary, to focus our lives — our time, our talents, and our means — on those matters that will make for the greatest good.

The Lord Jehovah spoke to Jeremiah of the sin of ancient Israel: "My people have committed two evils; they have forsaken me the fountain of living waters, and hewed them out cisterns, broken cisterns, that can hold no water." (Jeremiah 2:13.) It is a most serious matter to forsake the Lord, to ignore or reject his counsel, to turn a deaf ear to his divine direction. The Lord is the Way, and those who refuse his message thereby enter the broad road that leads to destruction. The

Lord is the Truth, and those who spurn his teachings and authority wander in ignorance. The Lord is the Life, and those who feel no need to align themselves with his will enter into league with him who seeks our spiritual death. The Lord is the Light, and those who forsake him choose in that action to walk in darkness. To forsake the Fountain of Living Waters is to deny oneself access to that living liquid that is the only sure antidote to the world's desperate thirst. And, unfortunately, there is no relief to be found in digging our own cisterns, or even in adopting those of others, especially those cisterns that are at best deficient and at worst perverse, those, in the language of Jehovah, that can hold no water, those that provide no deliverance from this world's woes.

Troublesome Trends

C. S. Lewis, in his masterwork, *The Screwtape Letters,* has one of the archdevils, Screwtape, giving instruction to his nephew, Wormwood, about how to deceive those who call themselves Christians: "The real trouble about the set your patient is living in is that it is *merely* Christian. They all have individual interests, of course, but the bond remains mere Christianity. What we want, if men become Christians at all, is to keep them in the state of mind I call 'Christianity And.' You know—Christianity and the Crisis, Christianity and the New Psychology, Christianity and the New Order, Christianity and Faith Healing, Christianity and Psychical Research, Christianity and Vegetarianism, Christianity and Spelling Reform. If they must be Christians, let them at least be Christians with a difference. Substitute for the faith itself some Fashion with a Christian colouring. Work on their horror of the Same Old Thing." (*The Screwtape Letters,* pp. 115–16; italics in original.)

The devil doesn't need to get us to steal or lie or commit adultery, just undersell, understate, and underestimate the powers, appropriateness, and relevance of the gospel. One challenge we face in a world that is expanding dramatically in regard to information, discovery, and technology is to hold fast to that which is fundamental, to rivet ourselves to the simple. In many cases new discoveries have and will yet pave the way to the amelioration of human suffering and the removal of so many of life's struggles. But there are some things that never change, some things whose resolution is brought to pass only through divine intervention. Paul taught us that in Christ "dwelleth all the fulness of the Godhead bodily. And *ye are complete in him,* which is the head of all principality and power." (Colossians 2:9–10; italics added.)

One Christian writer explained:

"A pastor I know of was conducting a series of meetings in several churches in North and South Carolina. He was staying in the home of some close friends in Asheville and traveling each night to wherever he was speaking that evening.

"One night he was scheduled to speak at a church in Greenville, South Carolina, which is several hours from Asheville. Because he didn't have a car, some friends from Greenville offered to transport him to and from the meeting. When they arrived to pick him up, he bid farewell to his hosts and told them he hoped to be back by midnight or soon afterward.

"After ministering at the Greenville church, he stayed awhile to enjoy some fellowship and then rode back to Asheville. Approaching the house, he saw the porch light on and assumed his hosts would be prepared for his arrival because he had discussed the time of his return with them. As he got out of the car, he sent his driver on his way, saying, 'You must hurry. You have a long drive back. I'm sure they're prepared for me; I'll have no problem.'

"He felt the bitter cold of the winter night as he walked the long distance to the house. By the time he reached the porch, his nose and ears were already numb. He tapped gently on the door but no one answered. He tapped a little harder, and then even harder—but still no reply. Finally, concerned about the intense cold, he beat on the kitchen door and on a side window. But there was still no response.

"Frustrated and becoming colder by the moment, he decided to walk to a neighboring house so he could call and awaken his hosts. On the way he realized that knocking on someone's door after midnight wasn't a safe thing to do, so he decided to find a public telephone. It was as dark as it was cold, and the pastor wasn't familiar with the area. Consequently he walked for several miles. At one point he slipped in the wet grass growing beside the road and slid down a bank into two feet of water. Soaked and nearly frozen, he crawled back up to the road and walked farther until he finally saw a blinking motel light. He awakened the manager, who was gracious enough to let him use the telephone.

"The bedraggled pastor made the call and said to his sleepy host, 'I hate to disturb you, but I couldn't get anyone in the house to wake up. I'm several miles down the road at the motel. Could you come get me?'

"To which his host replied, 'My dear friend, you have a key in your overcoat pocket. Don't you remember? I gave it to you before you left.'

"The pastor reached into his pocket. Sure enough, there was the key.

"That true story illustrates the predicament of Christians who try to gain access to God's blessings through human means, all the while possessing Christ, who is the key to every spiritual blessing. He alone fulfills the deepest longings of our hearts and supplies every spiritual resource we need." (John MacArthur, Jr., *Our Sufficiency in Christ,* pp. 25–27.)

In our complex world we find people on every corner eager to provide solutions to modern man's troubles. Radio and television programs, newspaper columns, magazine articles, and individual and group seminars or workshops abound. They're everywhere! Some focus on the importance of self-discovery, of coming to know who we are and what marvelous possibilities exist for us. Others seem to have an obsession with self-esteem, an inordinate concern with being on a type of perpetual emotional high. There are those who insist that the answer to all personal problems lies deep within ourselves, that the key to understanding and correcting our attitudes and actions lies somewhere in our past. Especially popular in the last decade is the idea that dysfunctional relationships with parents or siblings or childhood friends or marriage partners have resulted in stilted and perverted views of the world, that our problems now are largely a product of how people have in the past mistreated us, and that we need to "work through" such relationships to wholeness. Underlying much of what we are witnessing today is a very telling philosophy, one that is less than obvious to most people — that deep-seated problems can be solved only by professional counselors in well-orchestrated therapeutic settings; that scripture study, prayer, forgiveness, repentance, and the ordinances of the priesthood are overly simplistic and thus inadequate to deal with today's difficult challenges.

I do not write these things in total ignorance. I was trained as a psychologist and have great regard for the discipline and field. I know that hundreds and thousands of people are helped each year by caring, prepared, and thoughtful counselors and psychotherapists. Having worked for a time as a counselor, I am also very much aware that certain kinds of mental or social-emotional problems result from a chemical imbalance or may require intensive therapy. My concern is that far too often we understate the importance of the love and power of Jesus Christ to remake and renovate the human personality. The Spirit of the Lord is remarkably therapeutic. The love of God, as expressed by and through the Holy Ghost, is above and beyond anything earthly; in dealing with deep-seated problems of anger or bitterness or pain, it transcends in importance anything we could create or generate of ourselves. The principle of forgiveness — both to be forgiven and to give freely of the same to others — is a transcendent power, one that can bring hope and peace to a soul long habituated in the course of sin or anger. My gravest concern is that, like the minister above, we have within our reach a key, a supernal key, which to some degree is unappreciated and thus almost unused by too many of us. I have a feeling that when it comes to solving our problems the Lord expects us to take the scriptures, the words of modern prophets, the guidance of the Holy Ghost, and the powers of the priesthood as seriously as we do the guides and canons and procedures of learned men and women.

Also prevalent in today's world is a preoccupation with success and excellence. Books and tapes and seminars abound. Counsel and advice and direction and charts and schemes and planners fill the land. To the degree that such things help us focus upon the tasks ahead or to be more effective in what needs to be done, they are commendable. To the degree, however, that our quest for success, our yearning for excellence, leads us to become fiercely competitive, or our desire for improvement results in a fixation upon externals, we are walking in slippery paths. Bruce C. Hafen has written in this regard:

"I am addressing primarily a need for perspective. I do not mean to diminish the value of serious commitments to personal achievement and responsibility. The willingness to strive and keep striving is at the heart of [the scriptural] message to us. But *the striving must be to find out God and to accept fully the experiences he knows will enlarge our souls. The trouble with modern pursuits of excellence is that they can become a striving to please other people, or at least to impress them or to seek their approval.* A desire for such approval is not all bad, especially among Church members, who generally reserve their approval for accomplishments having positive value. *But other people are not finally our judge, and making too much of either the affirmative or the adverse judgments of others can actually undermine our relationship with God and our development of sound values.*" (*The Broken Heart*, pp. 98–99; italics added.)

It is just so with regard to an inordinate stress upon goal setting and achievement. We should and must have goals in life, and certainly we should do what is appropriate and right to bring them to pass. But our personal goals need to be in harmony with the Lord's grand design for us and for all his children. Further, a too great or unhealthy emphasis in this area can become an obsession, resulting in insensitivity to people (who may need our assistance but who do not immediately contribute to goal fulfillment) or to those sudden, unexpected promptings of the Spirit (which just might be designed to lead us in unanticipated directions).

The power unto life and salvation is in Christ the Person;

his grace is sufficient to heal us if we yield and submit and rely. The Savior came to change human nature. Too often we attempt to solve our spiritual problems in our own way. One example is an effort to remake or redo our personality through some kind of personal behavior modification plan. We decide to work on a vice (or virtue) for a period of time, move to the next one for a specified period, and so on. That is essentially the plan that Benjamin Franklin used for self-improvement. It certainly has merit, especially inasmuch as it encourages us to do our best to alleviate the flaws in our character through facing our weaknesses and applying self-control. And yet, such an approach is terrestrial at best. I have tried to think of an analogy that would illustrate this approach. It would be like my stepping into a baptismal font with water up to my chest, and then having a person in authority suddenly drop one hundred Ping-Pong balls into the font and say: "Brother Millet, if you desire to be saved in the celestial kingdom, you will need to get all those Ping-Pong balls under the water at the same time!" Being a confident type, I respond: "Hey, no problem. I can handle it!" I work at it for hours, using my arms and legs and head. Success is near as I manage to immerse seventy-five, eighty, eighty-five, and even ninety balls at once. Then, in unexpected fashion, fifteen or twenty pop up out of the water. I groan and go back to work.

I believe our sins are something like that. It's not just impractical to try to change our lives this way: *it's impossible!* The Lord's way is so much more effective, so much less frustrating, and so much more satisfying. He calls upon us to be born again, to have our natures changed so that we will come in time to have no desire to engage in our old ways. He bids us to acknowledge our weakness and human limitations, acknowledge his power to renew and refine us, and acknowledge that such a transformation can come in and through him and in no other way. As we do our best to overcome the bad habits, pray with real intent, and lean on that arm that is mighty to save, we begin in time to notice changes in our nature. I once sat in an interview with a fine young man who really desired to be pure in heart. He said to me: "Bishop, I want to get my life in order. I want the Spirit to be with me, and so each night I take the time to list all my sins and all my problems to the Lord. I pray for his forgiveness and ask him for specific help to overcome each one." I commended the young man for his diligence and his desires. I then suggested lovingly that he might consider an alternative approach—to pray about his nature and his desires, to ask the Lord to make of him a new creature in Christ, to give him in time a clean heart and an educated conscience.

The Lord has a way of assisting us in our problems that may be quite different from the solutions offered in today's world. Elder Dallin H. Oaks has cautioned us as follows: "We can liken the various ways of the world to implements that can draw water from a worldly well. We need such implements. We can and do use them to make our way in the world.

"But while we are doing this, in our occupations, in our civic responsibilities, and in our work in other organizations, we must never forget the Savior's words, 'Whosoever drinketh of this water shall thirst again.' Only from Jesus Christ, the Lord and Savior of this world, can we obtain the living water whose partaker shall never thirst again, in whom it will be 'a well of water springing up into everlasting life.' And we do not obtain that water with worldly implements." (*The Lord's Way*, p. 14.)

The Only Sure Foundation

A quiet but real peace accompanies the decision to yield ourselves as instruments of the Lord. Furthermore, safety and security—spiritual maturity—come from being rooted and grounded in the religion of Jesus Christ. When we are settled in the faith, securely fastened to principles of truth and righteousness, we will not be wafted about by false educational ideas or the philosophies or vagaries of men and women who know not God or his ways. Indeed, as the apostle Paul wrote, the true church is built upon the foundation of apostles and prophets with Jesus Christ himself as the chief cornerstone. (See Ephesians 2:19–20.)

Every person builds a house, a house of faith. We do so knowingly or unknowingly. And every builder soon learns that a good building with bad foundations is worse than useless; it is dangerous. As one Christian writer has observed, "If the stability of buildings depends largely on their foundations, so does the stability of human lives. The search for personal security is a primal instinct, but many fail to find it today. Old familiar landmarks are being obliterated. Moral absolutes which were once thought to be eternal are being abandoned." (John Stott, *Life in Christ,* p. 22.) Thus our house of faith can be no more secure than the foundation upon which it is built. The foolish build upon the shifting sands of ethics and the marshlands of manmade philosophies and doctrines. The wise build upon the rock of revelation, heeding carefully the living oracles, lest they be "brought under condemnation . . . , and stumble and fall when the storms descend, and the winds blow, and the rains descend, and beat upon their house." (D&C 90:5.) All that we do as members of the Lord's church must be built upon a foundation of faith and testimony and conversion. When external supports fail us, then our hearts must be riveted on the things of the Spirit, those internal realities that provide the meaning, the perspective, and the sustenance for all else that matters in life.

A very old tradition among the Jews holds that during the early stages of construction of the second temple, the builders, by mistake, discarded the cornerstone. Centuries later, in the midst of a long day of debate, Jesus, seemingly drawing upon this tradition, spoke of the irony associated with ignoring or dismissing him and his message. "Did ye never read in the scriptures, The stone which the builders rejected, the same is become the head of the corner: this is the Lord's doing, and it is marvellous in our eyes?" (Matthew 21:42; compare Psalm 118:22–23; Acts 4:11.) Among the Nephites, Jacob prophesied: "I perceive by the workings of the Spirit which is in me, that by the stumbling of the Jews they will reject the stone upon which they might build and have safe foundation." (Jacob 4:15.)

The climax of Helaman's commission to his sons Nephi and Lehi contains the following admonition: "And now, my sons, remember, remember that it is upon the rock of our Redeemer, who is Christ, the Son of God, that ye must build your foundation; that when the devil shall send forth his mighty winds, yea, his shafts in the whirlwind, yea, when all his hail and his mighty storm shall beat upon you, it shall have no power over you to drag you down to the gulf of misery and endless wo, because of the rock upon which ye are built, which is a sure foundation, a foundation whereon if men build they cannot fall." (Helaman 5:12.)

Surely the supreme challenge of this life for those who aspire to Christian discipleship is to build our lives on Christ, to erect a house of faith, a divine domicile in which he and his Spirit would be pleased to dwell. There is safety from

Satan and his minions only in Christ. There is security only in his word and through his infinite and eternal power.

How, then, do we build on Christ? In a day when the winds are blowing and the waves beating upon our ship, how do we navigate our course safely into the peaceful harbor? What must we do to have our Savior pilot us through life's tempestuous seas? Amidst the babble of voices—enticing voices that threaten to lead us into forbidden paths or that beckon us to labor in secondary causes—how do the Saints of the Most High know the Way, live the Truth, and gain that Life which is abundant? The revelations and the prophets offer us some simple yet far-reaching suggestions:

1. *Treasure up his word.* The scriptures are the words of Christ. They contain the warnings and doctrinal teachings of those who were moved upon by the Holy Ghost and thus spoke with the tongue of angels. (See 2 Nephi 31:13; 32:1–3; 33:10.) To read and ponder them is to hear the voice of the Master. (See D&C 18:34–36.) Holy writ has been preserved to bring us to Christ and to establish us upon his doctrine. The man or woman who is a serious student of the revelations, who seeks diligently to know and apply scriptural precepts and principles—he or she can more readily see the hand of God and can also discern the handiwork of Lucifer. Such a person is more equipped to sift and sort through the sordid, more prepared to distinguish the divine from the diabolical, the sacred from the secular.

Mormon explained that "whosoever will may lay hold upon the word of God, which is quick and powerful, which shall divide asunder all the cunning and the snares and the wiles of the devil, and lead the man of Christ in a strait and narrow course across that everlasting gulf of misery which is prepared to engulf the wicked." (Helaman 3:29.) The word of God, especially that found in the canon of scripture, allows us to discern and expose those teachings or schools of thought that lead us on intellectual or spiritual detours, to cut through false educational ideas, and to discard spurious notions that may be pleasing to the carnal mind but are in fact destructive to the eternal soul. Further, those who search and study the institutional revelations open themselves more fully to that individual revelation which is promised. Elder Bruce R. McConkie explained to Church leaders that "however talented men may be in administrative matters; however eloquent they may be in expressing their views; however learned they may be in worldly things—they will be denied the sweet whisperings of the Spirit that might have been theirs unless they pay the price of studying, pondering, and praying about the scriptures." (Regional Representatives Seminar, 2 Apr. 1982; as cited in *Doctrines of the Restoration,* p. 238.) Those who are grounded and settled in truth, anchored to the Lord's word, are built upon the rock of Christ. Or, in Mormon's words, those men and women of Christ who manage to lay hold upon the word of God and follow the strait and narrow path, eventually "land their souls, yea, their immortal souls, at the right hand of God in the kingdom of heaven, to sit down with Abraham, and Isaac, and with Jacob, and with all our holy fathers, to go no more out." (Helaman 3:30.)

2. *Teach his doctrine.* A supernal power accompanies the plain and direct teaching of doctrine. The views and philosophies of men—no matter how pleasingly they are stated or how lofty and timely they may seem—simply cannot engage the soul in the way the doctrines of the gospel can. If we teach doctrine, particularly the doctrine of Christ, and if we do so with the power and persuasion of the Holy Ghost, our listeners will be turned to Christ. "True doctrine, under-

stood," Elder Boyd K. Packer has taught, "changes attitudes
and behavior. The study of the doctrines of the gospel will
improve behavior quicker than a study of behavior will improve behavior. . . . That is why we stress so forcefully the
study of the doctrines of the gospel." (In Conference Report,
Oct. 1986, p. 20.)

3. *Sustain his servants.* The Savior taught his apostles in
the eastern hemisphere: "He that receiveth you receiveth me,
and he that receiveth me receiveth him that sent me." (Matthew 10:40.) To the Nephites the resurrected Lord said,
"Blessed are ye if ye shall give heed unto the words of these
twelve whom I have chosen from among you to minister unto
you, and to be your servants." (3 Nephi 12:1.) To receive the
apostles meant to accept them as the mouthpiece of deity,
recognizing their voice as his voice and their authority as his
authority. One certainly could not accept the Father while
rejecting the Son, and one could not accept the Son while
rejecting those he had commissioned to act in his name. A
rejection of Peter, James, Nephi, or any of his apostolic ministers was at the same time a rejection of Jesus.

There are those who feel they can enjoy a relationship
with the Lord independent of his Church, separate and apart
from the organization established by revelation. There are
even those who feel they can stay close to the Lord while
they criticize or find fault with the Church and its leaders.
These are wrong. They are deceived. They are painfully mis-
taken and are walking in slippery paths. No person comes to
the Master who does not acknowledge the mantle worn by
his anointed. There is no power to be found in Christ independent of his constituted priesthood authorities. In the
words of Elder Marvin J. Ashton, "Any Church member not
obedient to the leaders of this Church will not have the

opportunity to be obedient to the promptings of the Lord." (In Germany Area Conference Report, Aug. 1973, p. 23.)

4. *Trust in the Lord. Rely upon him.* There is power in Christ, power not only to create the worlds and divide the seas but also to still the storms of the human heart, to heal the pain of scarred and beaten souls. We must learn to trust in him more, in the arm of flesh less. We must learn to rely on him more, on manmade solutions less. We must learn to surrender our burdens more. We must learn to work to our limits and then be willing to seek that grace, or enabling power, which will make up the difference, that consummate power which indeed makes all the difference.

Few gifts of the Spirit are of greater worth in a day of doubt and a time of confusion than the gift of discernment. We have the challenge not only of discerning good from evil, light from darkness, but also of discerning that which matters from that which has but little value. In a time like our own when a babble of voices is heard, when discordant voices vie for our attention and seek for our time and interest, it is incumbent upon us to be discerning, to be discriminating. Some things simply matter more than others. But, in the words of Alma, "there is one thing which is of more impor- tance than they all." (Alma 7:7.) That something is the knowl- edge and testimony of Jesus, the calm certitude that comes by the spirit of revelation. We may know many things, but if we do not know this, our testimony is deficient and our foun- dation less solid than it might otherwise be. "Upon this rock," the rock of revelation, the Master said at Caesarea Philippi, "I will build my church." (Matthew 16:18; see also *Teachings of the Prophet Joseph Smith*, p. 274.) "And how could it be otherwise?" Elder Bruce R. McConkie asked. "There is no other foundation upon which the Lord could build his Church and kingdom. The things of God are known only by the power of his Spirit. God stands revealed or he remains forever unknown. No man can know that Jesus is the Lord but by the Holy Ghost.

"*Revelation:* Pure, perfect, personal revelation — this is the rock!

"*Revelation that Jesus is the Christ:* the plain, wondrous word that comes from God in heaven to man on earth, the word that affirms the divine Sonship of our Lord — this is the rock!

"*The divine sonship of our Lord:* the sure, heaven-sent word that God is his Father and that he has brought life and immortality to light through the gospel — this is the rock!

"*The testimony of our Lord:* the testimony of Jesus, which is the spirit of prophecy — this is the rock!

"All this is the rock, and yet there is more. *Christ is the Rock:* the Rock of Ages, the Stone of Israel, the Sure Foundation — the Lord Is our Rock!" (In Conference Report, Apr. 1981, pp. 102–3; italics in original.)

Truly, as the apostle Paul testified: "Other foundation can no man lay than that is laid, which is Jesus Christ." (1 Corinthians 3:11.) This message is certainly sounded clearly in scripture, but it is also echoed in hymns of faith and praise. Consider the following words by Edward Mote (as cited in John Stott, *Life in Christ,* p. 29):

> My hope is built on nothing less
> than Jesus' blood and righteousness;
> no merit of my own I claim,
> but wholly trust in Jesus' name.
>   On Christ, the solid rock, I stand —
>   all other ground is sinking sand.

When weary in this earthly race,
I rest on his unchanging grace;
in every wild and stormy gale
my anchor holds and will not fail.

His vow, his covenant and blood
are my defence against the flood;
when earthly hopes are swept away
he will uphold me on that day.

When the last trumpet's voice shall sound,
O may I then in him be found!
clothed in his righteousness alone,
faultless to stand before his throne.
   On Christ, the solid rock, I stand —
all other ground is sinking sand.

Ponder the significance of the words of a hymn we frequently sing:

How firm a foundation, ye Saints of the Lord,
Is laid for your faith in his excellent word!
What more can he say than to you he hath said,
Who unto the Savior for refuge have fled?

. . . .

When through fiery trials thy pathway shall lie,
My grace, all sufficient, shall be thy supply.
The flame shall not hurt thee; I only design
Thy dross to consume and thy gold to refine.

E'en down to old age, all my people shall prove
My sov'reign, eternal, unchangeable love;
And then, when gray hair shall their temples adorn,
Like lambs shall they still in my bosom be borne.

The soul that on Jesus hath leaned for repose
I will not, I cannot, desert to his foes;
That soul, though all hell should endeavor to shake,
I'll never, no never, no never forsake!
(*Hymns,* 1985, no. 85.)

Elder Marion D. Hanks has explained: "A perusal of the Christian's passageway seems almost too much. How can ordinary mortals walk it? If we are to regard our religion as a 'packet of beliefs and practices' to be borne, it will indeed be too much. But this cannot be for the Christian. Our religion is 'not weight; it is wings.' It can carry us through the dark times, the bitter cup. It will be with us in the fiery furnace and deep pit. It will accompany us to the hospital room and to the graveside. It can assure us of the presence of a captain on the rough voyage. It is, in short, not the path to easy disposition of problems but the comforting assurance of the eternal light by which we may see and the eternal warmth that we may feel. All of this comes to us through the love of Christ." (*Bread upon the Waters,* p. 34.)

President Spencer W. Kimball spoke to the Saints of the need for holding tenaciously to the truth, of grounding ourselves in gospel verities. "The forces of good are clearly and continually under attack," he said. "There are times when it seems the world is almost drowning in a flood of filth and degradation. And I want to cry out, 'Hold on! Hold on to what is right and true. Therein is safety. Don't let yourself be swept away.'

"In 1946 I visited Hawaii shortly after a huge tidal wave, where walls of water some forty feet high struck Hilo and the Hamakua coast, and I saw the devastation that resulted. Homes had been overturned and shredded, crushed into splinters like toothpicks; fences and gardens were obliterated; bridges and roads were washed away. Bathtubs, refrigerators, mangled autos lay strewn all about the streets. Where one of our little chapels had stood, nothing remained but the foundation. More than a hundred people lost their lives; as many more were injured; thousands were left homeless. I heard many stories while there of suffering, of heroism, of salvation.

"One woman told how she received a telephone message from friends to get out and to leave — that a tidal wave was coming. She looked out to sea and saw the monstrous wave approaching, like a mountain. She and her husband picked up the baby and ran for their lives up the hill. However, two of their little girls were away from home playing near a clump of lauhala trees. They saw the wave coming, ran into the trees, and held tightly with their arms around the tree trunks. The first gigantic wave washed entirely over them, but they held their breath and clung with all their might until the water receded and their heads were again above the water. When the wave receded, they quickly ran up the hill before the succeeding waves came. Together, the family watched from the safety of the hill as their home below disappeared under the pounding of the waves.

"We, too, are faced with powerful, destructive forces unleashed by the adversary. Waves of sin, wickedness, immorality, degradation, tyranny, deceitfulness, conspiracy, and dishonesty threaten all of us. They come with great power and speed and will destroy us if we are not watchful.

"But a warning is sounded for us. It behooves us to be alert and to listen and flee from the evil for our eternal lives. Without help we cannot stand against it. We must flee to high ground or cling fast to that which can keep us from being swept away. That to which we must cling for safety is the gospel of Jesus Christ. It is our protection from whatever force the evil one can muster. (In Conference Report, Oct. 1978, pp. 5–6.)

As we continue in his word, as we move forward in steadfast but unsensational fashion, as we come to live by every word of God, we come to know him who is the Truth: we come to know our Lord. We come to know about the Lord by study. We come to know the Lord only by study in combination with faith. Jesus said: "I am the way, the truth, and the life: no man cometh unto the Father, but by me." (John 14:6.) It is not just that the Son of God brought light into a darkened and fallen world; he *is* the light. (3 Nephi 11:11.) It is not just that our Savior showed us the way; he *is* the way. (John 14:6.) It is not just that Christ made the resurrection available; he *is* the resurrection. (John 11:25.) And it is not just that Jesus of Nazareth restored the truth and taught the truth; he *is* the truth. (John 14:6.) Knowing these things, knowing that our hope for peace here and our longing for eternal glory hereafter are inextricably tied to Jesus Christ, we gladly acknowledge him as our Lord and God, our King Emmanuel, truly the Hope of Israel.

Epilogue

When I first was given the assignment to direct the institute of religion connected with Florida State University, I became acquainted with a young college student who had just joined the Church. David was a ball of fire, an enthusiastic, missionary-minded convert who was also like a sponge as far as knowledge and understanding were concerned. He just couldn't get enough! He attended every institute class. He would sit back, read the scriptures with us, and, at the moment of discovery of some new principle or insight, get a glow in his eyes, and let out a "Wow!" or "Oooh!" or "I can't believe it!" Such outbursts were at first humorous to the other students but over time came to be a regular part of the class experience. It was fun to watch David grow and, more important, to sense his deep appreciation for the marvelous light and truth which flow from the restored gospel. A year after his baptism David left on a mission, and things quieted down in my classes substantially.

His homecoming address was most inspirational. Before us stood a young man who had come to know the Lord, who had gained a closeness to the Lord's Spirit, and who would be a staunch defender of the Lord's church and kingdom.

We all noticed in institute class that David made few comments and seldom if ever responded in his typical enthusiastic manner to points of interest. No grunts, no shouts, no gesticulations. Just an occasional smile and a nod of the head. After a few months David asked to speak with me privately. In our interview he expressed a personal fear that he had lost something. "I just don't seem to be as excited as I once was about the gospel." I asked: "Is that because you seem to be having fewer 'Ah hah' experiences?" He nodded. I explained the very fundamental principle that the depth of our spiritual maturity is not necessarily to be measured by what shows, by decibels of delight or brand new doctrinal discoveries or how high our spiritual high may be today. Rather, as we move along that path which the scriptures describe as strait and narrow, we actually become more stable and secure, less prone perhaps to unnatural spiritual highs or abyssmal lows. As the Holy Ghost transforms our soul, as we begin to forsake the world and find delight in the noble and uplifting, we begin to enjoy the quiet assurance that God is in his heaven, that the work in which we are engaged is true and will triumph, and finally (but more important) that the Holy One is pleased with our offerings. Our testimony of the truth becomes stronger and stronger, but our desire to share it and our feelings of appreciation for what matters are more often couched in the simple expressions of testimony and gratitude. Though we know more surely than we have ever known, though the scriptures and the words of the living
ᵃcles have become manna to our taste, though our desire
ᵗclaim the truths of the gospel knows no bounds, yet
has been tempered by wisdom and our enthusiasm
d a dignity and a stability that characterize those
ᵗadfast and immovable.

The present thrust of the Church toward simplification and reduction is an inspired one. It causes us to reexamine our lives, evaluate our motives and priorities, and direct our efforts toward those things of greatest worth. One antidote to complexity and confusion is a renewed focus on fundamentals. As we spend our time and our resources on the things that lead us to God and cause us to love and reach out to his children, we are on the road to gospel greatness. "After all," President Joseph F. Smith observed, *"to do well those things which God ordained to be the common lot of all man-kind, is the truest greatness. . . .*

"We should never be discouraged in those daily tasks which God has ordained to the common lot of man. Each day's labor should be undertaken in a joyous spirit and with the thought and conviction that our happiness and eternal welfare depend upon doing well that which we ought to do, that which God has made it our duty to do. . . .

"Let us not be trying to substitute an artificial life for the true one. He is truly happy who can see and appreciate the beauty with which God has adorned the commonplace things of life." (*Gospel Doctrine,* pp. 285–86; italics added.)

In many ways, the gospel of Jesus Christ is one of the best-kept secrets in the Church. I refer not necessarily to the knowledge and understanding associated with the gospel but rather to the gospel as an experience, as "the power of God unto salvation." (Romans 1:16.) We are too often prone to be content with traveling about in twilight when we could walk and talk in the glorious light of the noonday sun. (See D&C 95:5–6.) In short, we have within easy reach the powers of God, but because of preoccupation or distraction we fail to appropriate such endowments into our lives. In so doing, we fall short of that spiritual maturity that might otherwise be ours. At a time when the early Latter-day Saints were struggling under financial pressures, the Lord provided what we might call the "vertical dimension of problem solving." He said: "And again, verily I say unto you, concerning your debts—behold it is my will that you shall pay all your debts. And it is my will that you shall humble yourselves before me, and obtain this blessing by your diligence and humility and the prayer of faith. And inasmuch as you are diligent and humble, and exercise the prayer of faith, behold, I will soften the hearts of those to whom you are in debt, until I shall send means unto you for your deliverance." (D&C 104:78–80.) The Lord stands ready to assist us; the depth of our sincerity and our maturity may be discerned by the degree to which we are willing to trust him.

The story is told of a poor man who had always wanted to go on a cruise. "As a youngster he had seen an advertisement for a luxury cruise, and ever since, he had dreamed of spending a week on a large ocean liner enjoying fresh sea air and relaxing in a luxurious environment. He saved money for years, carefully counting his pennies, often sacrificing personal needs so he could stretch his resources a little further.

"Finally he had enough to purchase a cruise ticket. He went to a travel agent, looked over the cruise brochures, picked out one that was especially attractive, and bought a ticket with the money he had saved so long. He was hardly able to believe he was about to realize his childhood dream.

"Knowing he could not afford the kind of elegant food pictured in the brochure, the man planned to bring his own provisions for the week. Accustomed to moderation after years of frugal living, and with his entire savings going to pay for the cruise ticket, the man decided to bring along a week's supply of bread and peanut butter. That was all he could afford.

"The first few days of the cruise were thrilling. The man ate peanut-butter sandwiches alone in his room each morning and spent the rest of his time relaxing in the sunlight and fresh air, delighted to be aboard ship.

"By midweek, however, the man was beginning to notice that he was the only person on board who was not eating luxurious meals. It seemed that every time he sat on the deck or rested in the lounge or stepped outside his cabin, a porter would walk by with a huge meal for someone who had ordered room service.

"By the fifth day of the cruise the man could take it no longer. The peanut-butter sandwiches seemed stale and tasteless. He was desperately hungry, and even the fresh air and sunshine had lost their appeal. Finally, he stopped a porter and exclaimed, 'Tell me how I might get one of those meals! I'm dying for some decent food, and I'll do anything you say to earn it!'

" 'Why, sir, don't you have a ticket for this cruise?' the porter asked.

" 'Certainly,' said the man. 'But I spent everything I had for that ticket. I have nothing left with which to buy food.'

" 'But sir,' said the porter, 'didn't you realize? Meals are included with your passage. You may eat as much as you like!' " (John MacArthur, Jr., *Our Sufficiency in Christ,* pp. 241–42.)

Too often we are like the man on the cruise: we have unlimited possibilities for growth and development, infinite avenues for joy and contentment, all available through the omniloving offering and gift of our Lord and Master Jesus Christ. But we settle for less. Much, much less. Surely one sign of spiritual maturity is the ability to recognize a good deal when it presents itself to us and then to clinch it!

We have discussed several aspects of gospel living that contribute to our spiritual maturity. As we learn to respond appropriately to the questions that arise in our lives; as we pursue a sane and balanced course in life, stay in the mainstream of the Church and move toward our eternal goals with dignity and patient maturity; as we seek gospel growth through consistent and steady personal study; as we acquire and bear that pure testimony which is reflected so often in the utterances of the Lord's anointed; as we plead with all the energy of our souls for that love of God which transforms the human personality and all human interactions; as we come to trust in and rely on the merits, mercy, and grace of the Holy Messiah, thus looking unto God that we might live (Alma 37:47) — as we do these things, we begin to build our houses of faith upon the rock of our Redeemer. We lay the foundation for a life in which we will be, even in the midst of adversity and turmoil, steadfast and immovable. Through this means we gain in time the transcendent assurance that the Lord is pleased with us, that eternal life is at the end of our course. "Therefore, my beloved brethren," Paul wrote, "be ye stedfast, unmoveable, always abounding in the work of the Lord, forasmuch as ye know that your labour is not in vain in the Lord." (1 Corinthians 15:58.) Indeed, King Benjamin's challenge and invitation are ever before us: "Therefore, I would that ye should be steadfast and immovable, always abounding in good works, that Christ, the Lord God Omnipotent, may seal you his, that you may be brought to heaven, that ye may have everlasting salvation and eternal life, through the wisdom, and power, and justice, and mercy of him who created all things, in heaven and in earth, who is God above all. Amen." (Mosiah 5:15.)

Bibliography

Ashton, Marvin J. In Germany Area Conference Report, August 1973, pp. 22–23.

Backman, Milton V., Jr. *Joseph Smith's First Vision: Confirming Evidences and Contemporary Accounts.* 2d ed. Salt Lake City: Bookcraft, 1980.

Benson, Ezra Taft. *Come unto Christ.* Salt Lake City: Deseret Book Co., 1983.

——. *The Teachings of Ezra Taft Benson.* Salt Lake City: Bookcraft, 1988.

Cannon, George Q. *Gospel Truth.* 2 vols. in 1. Sel. Jerreld L. Newquist. Salt Lake City: Deseret Book Co., 1987.

Clark, James R., comp. *Messages of the First Presidency of The Church of Jesus Christ of Latter-day Saints.* 6 vols. Salt Lake City: Bookcraft, 1965–75.

Conference Report. Salt Lake City: The Church of Jesus Christ of Latter-day Saints, April 1965; April 1970; October 1972; April 1977; October 1977; April 1981; April 1985; October 1985; October 1986; October 1987; October 1988; October 1989.

Cowley, Matthew. *Matthew Cowley Speaks: Discourses of Elder Matthew Cowley of the Quorum of the Twelve of the Church of Jesus Christ of Latter-day Saints.* Salt Lake City: Deseret Book Co., 1971.

Dostoyevsky, Fyodor. *The Brothers Karamazov.* Translated by David Magarshack. New York: Penguin Books, 1982.

George, Bob. *Classic Christianity.* Eugene, Oregon: Harvest House Publishers, 1989.

Hafen, Bruce C. *The Broken Heart: Applying the Atonement to Life's Experiences.* Salt Lake City: Deseret Book Co., 1989.

Hanks, Marion D. *Bread upon the Waters.* Salt Lake City: Bookcraft, 1991.

Hunter, Howard W. "Eternal Investments." Address to CES personnel, Salt Lake City, 10 February 1989.

Hymns of The Church of Jesus Christ of Latter-day Saints. Salt Lake City: Corporation of the President of The Church of Jesus Christ of Latter-day Saints, 1985.

Kimball, Spencer W. *Faith Precedes the Miracle.* Salt Lake City: Deseret Book Co., 1974.

———. *The Teachings of Spencer W. Kimball.* Edited by Edward L. Kimball. Salt Lake City: Bookcraft, 1982.

Lee, Harold B. *Stand Ye in Holy Places: Selected Sermons and Writings of President Harold B. Lee.* Salt Lake City: Deseret Book Co., 1974.

———. "Be Loyal to the Royal within You." *Brigham Young University Speeches of the Year, 1973.* Provo, Utah: Brigham Young University Publications, 1974.

———. "The Day in Which We Live." *Improvement Era,* June 1970, pp. 28–30.

———. "To the Defenders of the Faith." *Improvement Era,* June 1970, pp. 63–65.

Lewis, C. S. *Mere Christianity.* New York: Macmillan Publishing Co., 1952.

———. *The Screwtape Letters.* New York: Macmillan Publishing Co., 1961.

MacArthur, John, Jr. *Our Sufficiency in Christ.* Dallas: Word Publishing, 1991.

McConkie, Bruce R. *Doctrines of the Restoration.* Edited by Mark L. McConkie. Salt Lake City: Bookcraft, 1989.

———. *The Promised Messiah.* Salt Lake City: Deseret Book Co., 1978.

———. "What Think Ye of Salvation by Grace?" *Brigham Young University 1983–84 Fireside and Devotional Speeches.* Provo, Utah: Brigham Young University Publications, 1984.

McConkie, Joseph F., and Robert L. Millet. *The Holy Ghost.* Salt Lake City: Bookcraft, 1989.

McKay, David O. *Gospel Ideals: Selections from the Discourses of David O. McKay.* Salt Lake City: Improvement Era, 1953.

Millennial Star. Liverpool, England. April 1894.

Millet, Robert L. *An Eye Single to the Glory of God: Reflections on the Cost of Discipleship.* Salt Lake City: Deseret Book Co., 1991.

Oaks, Dallin H. *The Lord's Way.* Salt Lake City: Deseret Book Co., 1991.

———. "Family History: 'In Wisdom and Order.' " *Ensign,* June 1989, pp. 6–8.

Packer, Boyd K. *Teach Ye Diligently.* Salt Lake City: Deseret Book Co., 1975.

———. *"That All May Be Edified": Talks, Sermons, and Commentary by Boyd K. Packer.* Salt Lake City: Bookcraft, 1982.

———. *Follow the Brethren.* Provo, Utah: Brigham Young University Publications, 1965.

Robinson, Stephen E. "Believing Christ." *Brigham Young University 1989–90 Devotional and Fireside Speeches.* Provo, Utah: Brigham Young University Publications, 1990.

Smith, Joseph F. *Gospel Doctrine: Selections from the Sermons and Writings of Joseph F. Smith.* Salt Lake City: Deseret Book Co., 1971.

Smith, Joseph, Jr. *Teachings of the Prophet Joseph Smith.* Sel. Joseph Fielding Smith. Salt Lake City: Deseret Book Co., 1976.

Stoker, H. Stephen, and Joseph C. Muren, comps. *Testimony.* Salt Lake City: Bookcraft, 1980.

Stott, John. *Life in Christ.* Wheaton, Ill.: Tyndale House Publishers, 1991.

Swindoll, Charles. *The Grace Awakening.* Dallas: Word Publishing, 1990.

Whitney, Orson F. *Life of Heber C. Kimball.* 4th ed. Salt Lake City: Bookcraft, 1973.

Widtsoe, John A. *Evidences and Reconciliations,* arr. G. Homer Durham. Salt Lake City: Bookcraft, 1987.

Index

Winder, John R., 47–48
Witness: of God and Jesus
   Christ, 54–57, 72; of the
   truth, 70; of Joseph Smith, 72
Word of Wisdom, observance of
   the, 26

Works, importance of, 119
World, ways of the, 139

Zeal, excessive, 25–26
Zion, 104